# Feminism after Postmodernism

What has happened to feminism over the last few decades? Is it any use as a 'politics for women' any more? Or has feminism lost its political edge and utility having changed beyond all recognition since the massive influence of postmodern and poststructural ideas? This book addresses these questions, and presents a valuable overview of the main forms of feminism at the heart of the traditional/contemporary or modernist/postmodernist debate.

In order to 'think the theories through practice', Zalewski uses the example of reproductive technologies (such as IVF, amniocentesis and ultrasound), which unexpectedly reveals some intriguing similarities between modernist and postmodernist feminisms and illustrates some of the beneficial legacies of the more traditional feminisms, casting doubt on claims that such feminisms are anachronistic.

Engagingly written, *Feminism after Postmodernism* is an essential guide for all those working in gender studies and feminist theory.

**Marysia Zalewski** teaches in the Centre for Women's Studies, Queen's University, Belfast. She is co-editor of *The 'Man' Question in International Relations, International Theory: Positivism and Beyond*, and is co-conversations editor of *International Feminist Journal of Politics*, published by Routledge.

# Feminism after Postmodernism

Theorising through practice

**Marysia Zalewski**

London and New York

First published 2000 by Routledge
11 New Fetter Lane, London EC4P 4EE

Simultaneously published in the USA and Canada
by Routledge
29 West 35th Street, New York, NY 10001

*Routledge is an imprint of the Taylor & Francis Group*

© 2000 Marysia Zalewski

Typeset in Times by BC Typesetting, Bristol
Printed and bound in Great Britain by Clays Ltd, St Ives plc

*British Library Cataloguing in Publication Data*
A catalogue record for this book is available from the
British Library

*Library of Congress Cataloging in Publication Data*
Zalewski, Marysia.
 Feminism after postmodernism: theorising through practice/
Marysia Zalewski
  p. cm
Includes bibliographical references and index.
1. Feminist theory. 2. Feminism – Philosophy.
3. Reproductive technology – Philosophy.
I. Title.
HQ1190.Z35 2000
305.42′01–dc21                              00-036600

ISBN 0–415–20238–8 (hbk)
ISBN 0–415–23461–1 (pbk)

**for cindy**

# Contents

*Preface*                                                           ix
*Acknowledgements*                                                  xii

1  Introduction: different feminist theories                        1

2  The gulf: theoretical differences                               29

3  Modernist feminisms and reproductive technologies:
   thinking theory through practice                                75

4  Postmodernist feminisms and reproductive
   technologies: thinking theory through practice                 105

5  'Recovering' feminisms?                                         128

   *Glossary of medical terms*                                     143
   *References*                                                    148
   *Index*                                                         157

# Preface

Over the last decade or so, a number of feminists have argued that a gulf or huge chasm-like gap exists between the feminisms typically associated with the 1970s (commonly thought of as modernist or traditional feminisms) and those associated with the 1990s (postmodernist or contemporary feminisms).[1] This book takes on and challenges the idea that there is such a gulf. It is important to address this notion of a gulf between these feminisms because it raises the question of how to 'do' feminist politics. The alleged chasm between modernist feminisms and postmodernist feminisms has resulted in each group questioning the politics of the other. Modernist feminists have typically declared postmodern feminisms apolitical and therefore useless for feminism, while postmodern feminists have dismissed more traditional feminisms as anachronistic and virtually useless. In this book I take on these arguments and their implications, not only theoretically, but through a specific set of practices – reproductive technologies – in order to illustrate why it matters that there might be significant differences between feminist theories.

In the first chapter I introduce the idea of a gulf between traditional or modernist feminisms and postmodern feminisms by imagining a conversation between two well-known feminists: Andrea Dworkin and Judith Butler. 'Would they agree on anything?', I ask, in order to start illustrating how differently feminists might think. My aim in this chapter is to start explaining what some of the differences between feminist theories are. As such, I introduce some of the key themes and ideas from the four central categories of feminist thought which are the key 'players' in the alleged gulf between modernist feminisms and postmodernist feminisms: liberal, radical, socialist and postmodern.

In Chapter 2 I go into more theoretical detail about the nature of the alleged gulf. I organise this discussion around three keys issues: the (human) subject; epistemology (theories of and questions about knowledge); and the nature of politics and political action. These are three areas where there appear to be significant differences between modernist and postmodernist feminisms. I suggest that the fear and emotion involved in debates about these differences between modernist and postmodernist feminists indicate that something rather important is at stake in the idea that there is a chasm between them. I introduce my discussion about the subject, politics and epistemology by introducing and discussing three of the biggest fears which are as follows.

*Modernists on postmodernists*

- Postmodernists have abandoned all belief in the subject, which means that claims for rights on behalf of subjects cannot be made.
- Postmodernists deny there is a 'real truth'. If this is the case how can anyone ever prove anything is right or wrong?
- Postmodernism cannot provide an agenda for political action and it is apolitical or even anti-political.

*Postmodernist responses to those fears*

- Modernists are under the illusion that there are real, a priori subjects on which to make claims to rights.
- Modernists are under the illusion that there is a 'real truth' out there waiting to be discovered.
- Modernists are under the illusion that it is possible to have sure grounds for political action.

I take each of these fears and responses and outline typical modernist feminist views and postmodernist feminist views on each. I end the chapter with a discussion about whether there is evidence of a gulf between modernist and postmodern feminisms.

My aim is not to suggest that we have to think that feminist theory over the last few decades has followed a rigid progressive pattern – modernist then postmodernist. However, it is the case that the debate about a gulf has been presented in this chronological way and so in order to interrogate and challenge it, it is necessary to introduce and discuss it on its own terms in the first instance. Ultimately however, the idea of a progressive chronology is something I want to question.

I also do not wish to give the impression that there is *one* modernist or *one* postmodernist feminist story about anything. My aim in this book is to give an idea of the differences between these feminisms and as such I suggest typical ways that modernist feminists or post-

modern feminists might think about certain issues. Given the nature of
the debate about modernist versus postmodernist feminisms over the
last few decades, it clearly must be the case that many feminists believe
there are some things that distinguish these feminisms from each other.
It is my aim in this book to find out what these differences are and to
interrogate their significance.

In the next two chapters I focus on the practices of reproductive technologies by introducing some of the stories told about these practices
by theories of modernist and postmodernist feminisms. I look at reproductive technologies through the three main categories I introduced in
Chapter 2: the subject, epistemology and politics. A question I frequently use in these chapters is: 'In the face of what is, what should
we do?' (Price, 1997: 34). If feminisms are as different as the idea of
a gulf implies, then this would indicate that different feminisms will
inspire different answers or ways to approach both the question of
'what is' and 'what should we do?' In order to address these questions
and issues, throughout the chapter I use several images or stories
invoked by the use of reproductive technologies.

In the final chapter I return to the central questions raised by the
discussions in the book. These include:

• What is the nature of the gulf between modernist and postmodernist feminisms?
• How is it that each of these bodies of feminist thought has been
  declared 'useless' by the other?
• Why do the differences between feminist theories matter?
• How might we think of or use feminism – in theory and in practice –
  in the twenty-first century?

**Note**

1 The debate I refer to is a specifically Western feminist debate and the
  feminist writers involved are generally Anglo-American.

# Acknowledgements

I am indebted to many people for their support and encouragement – personal and intellectual – over the last few years in which this book has been completed. To name some of them: Helen Brocklehurst, Berenice Carroll, Cynthia Enloe, Simon Murden, Palena Neale, Spike Peterson, Jindy Pettman, Susan Roberts, Fiona Sampson, Hazel Smith and Gillian Youngs. As always, the support from the members of the British International Studies Association gender group as well as from the International Studies Association feminist and gender section has proved invaluable.

Most of the work for this book was completed while I was at the University of Wales, Aberystwyth – though it was at Queen's University in Belfast that the book was finally completed. I am grateful to the University of Wales for a grant awarded to me to carry out research for this project in 1997.

The care and presence of my daughters, Tessa and Laura, as well as my parents are a constant reminder of what is really important in my life, and I thank them for that. This book is dedicated to Cynthia Weber, who has lived with this project – and all that went alongside it – through its various reincarnations and guises. We are both now very happy that the specific form of dedication is now a lived one.

Marysia Zalewski
Belfast, March 2000

# 1 Introduction
## Different feminist theories

Imagine Andrea Dworkin and Judith Butler in conversation about feminism. Would they, could they, agree on anything? Think, for example, about a conversation between them on male violence towards women. How can we imagine the conversation going? Would Andrea Dworkin speak about a 'war against women'? Or about a continuum of male violence from the cradle to the grave; from the bedroom to the boardroom? And would Judith Butler resist such terms and instead question the authority of those who claim that they can speak on behalf of such a disparate group called 'women'?

Imagine a discussion between them on the question of what feminism is or what women are. Butler might speak not only of the impossibility of reaching such definitions but also of the dangers of definitional practices and instead suggest that we look at the effects of those practices. However, Dworkin might respond that, despite the difficulties, it is vital to hold on to some clear views about what women are and what they want or what the demands of feminism are. To abandon such clarity threatens to lead us into a feminist nightmare where we cannot speak of women at all or feel confident in using feminist politics to demand rights and freedoms for women.

Why imagine this conversation? Why is it important to wonder about whether Andrea Dworkin and Judith Butler might agree on feminist issues? What is at stake?

I am introducing this book through this imagined conversation between Andrea Dworkin and Judith Butler partly because these two writers seem to embody two *apparently* opposing bodies of feminist thought. Dworkin would for many be seen as the quintessential 1970s radical feminist, with Butler being the paradigm of a contemporary postmodern feminist. In fact both of these writers seem to stand as exemplary figures for the feminisms they are associated with – in the sense that each of these figures is frequently taken to pose as something of a 'warning to [feminist] others'[1] because of their paradigmatic status. One effect of this is that they seem to stand out as examples of the type of feminist 'you don't want to be', if you happen to disagree with their theoretical positions. Of course with Dworkin, this image of her as a paradigm of radical feminism has had some rather nasty consequences. It has always struck me as suspicious that she appears to be one of the most maligned feminists of the late twentieth century, especially as she is so often represented as the antithesis of what 'western patriarchal man' imagines woman should be. Dworkin is not pretty, she is fat and she refuses to shut up. Additionally, her feminist theory and politics still seem very much tethered to the unfashionable foundational claims and rhetorics of western feminisms typical of the 1970s. That is to say, she still speaks the language of 'universal woman', 'ubiquitous patriarchy', a 'war against women' and a continuum of male violence.

Judith Butler, on the other hand, eloquently speaks the rhetoric of the postmodern 1990s – refusing foundational claims, refusing to accept definitions ('Is there, after all, something called postmodernism?' [1995: 35]) and frequently resisting the form of questions put to her. Her apparent evasiveness about questions such as 'what feminism is' or 'who women are' has positioned her as a paradigm of a postmodern feminism which, for those fearful and suspicious of it, means all will be lost in the battle to demand rights on behalf of women, because women are simply a fiction. Interestingly, however, Butler too confounds 'western patriarchal man's' image of what a woman should be, as she is a lesbian.

What does all this imply for western feminism as we move into the twenty-first century? Does it really matter that Dworkin and Butler might approach or think about feminism differently to each other, or that the feminisms they are taken to represent are so different? What does this mean Dworkin and Butler actually *do* with their views on feminism or perhaps more pertinently what others might do with their ideas? Or in other words, towards what sort of political and/or practical actions do their differing ways of thinking about feminism lead? For example, do their theoretical positions inspire us to support the rights of minority groups or join 'reclaim the night marches'? Do they cause us to worry about the future for women? To cut to the crucial question, what do these ways of thinking about feminism allow, enable or inspire us to do?

Feminism seemed so much simpler a few decades ago! In 1983 Alison Jaggar comfortably claimed that 'all feminists address the same problem: what constitutes the oppression of women and how can that oppression be ended?' (1983: 124). This view seems misplaced in contemporary feminist debates. Does it matter that the consensus doesn't exist any more? Would we want to return to it? What are the consequences of a choice either way? The proliferation of feminisms over the last few decades has simply become too frustrating for some feminists. 'Contemporary feminist theory is a tangled and forbidding web . . . practising feminists . . . approach the proliferation of feminist theory with an acute sense of frustration' (Nye, 1988: 1). This sense of frustration has been exacerbated for many by the belief that approaches to feminism grouped under the label 'postmodern' have seemingly become dominant, so much so that modernist or 1970s feminisms have been declared 'virtually useless' (Gatens, 1992: 120) and 'anachronistic' (Coole, 1994: 129). In other words, the radical feminism of someone like Andrea Dworkin is old-fashioned and of little, if any, use in this new millennium.

This is a big claim to make. Can it really be accurate to say that the feminisms typical of the 1970s – liberal, Marxist/socialist and radical – are of no contemporary use? Are the differences between the feminisms of the 1970s and the 1990s so immense? For many contemporary feminist writers, the answer to the latter question is a resounding yes! The differences between 1970s and 1990s feminisms are so huge that some speak of an apparently unbridgeable 'gulf' (Barrett and Phillips, 1992: 2). Others, less dramatically, write of a 'theoretical shift' within feminism since the 1960s (Alcoff, 1997: 6); or a 'paradigm shift' (Brooks, 1997: 8). These writers have largely considered and discussed this so-called gulf at a theoretical level. What I do in this book is reconsider and re-evaluate the claim that there is a theoretical gulf by thinking how the theoretical differences are related to practice. One of the reasons it is important to think about theoretical differences in this way is because it will allow me to address the question 'How and in what ways do the differences between feminisms and feminists matter in the everyday?'

## Thinking theory through practice

### *Which theories?*

In order to take up my task of 'thinking theory through practice' and to address the issue of the everyday, I want to introduce the feminist theories that have been identified as being associated with or 'belonging to' the 1970s and the 1990s. As mentioned above, for the 1970s these are liberal, Marxist/socialist and radical, and for the 1990s, postmodern and poststructural. It is not my intention to reify these categories or to go through them in a boring and tedious way. However, I do need to extricate some of the key questions, issues and themes that have been identified as being part of these theories precisely in order to re-evaluate the idea that there is a huge gap between 1970s and 1990s feminisms. Anyone writing about feminism in the late 1990s has to be very reflective about the practice of categorising feminisms, a point to which I shall return to in Chapter 5. But it is the case that these categories of feminist thought have frequently and consistently been used by feminists. It is therefore important, in the first instance, to use them to help us understand why the differences between feminisms matter.

Also mentioned earlier, another way of framing this division is by calling 1970s feminisms 'modernist' and 1990s feminisms 'postmodernist'. You might note that this gathering together of the four big feminisms of the 1970s under the label of 'modernism' seems to imply that there are minimal differences between them. This seems to be another rather grand claim. Imagine a conversation between Andrea Dworkin and a liberal feminist such as Betty Friedan. How different might their feminist ideas and politics be? The grouping together of 1970s feminisms under the generic label of 'modernism' suggests that there are significant commonalities between them, or at least sufficient commonalities such that they can be considered together in opposition to the feminisms of the 1990s. This does seem somewhat strange, given the lengthy and serious debates between them, focusing on their differences, during the 1960s, 1970s and 1980s. I shall return to all these issues in Chapter 5.

### Which practice?

The area of practice I shall 'think theory through' is reproductive technologies. This is a good area to select for several reasons. One reason is that the feminisms of both the 1970s and 1990s have all expressed an interest in the uses, abuses and constructions of women's bodies, especially in the arena of reproduction. This means that I can ask questions about reproductive technologies from varying feminist perspectives, which will enable me to illustrate how different ways of thinking or theorising about feminism do or do not lead to different ways of thinking about or dealing with a practical issue. For example, if I am a liberal feminist dedicated to the principle of equal rights and opportunities for women especially in the public world of work, what will I think about the use of ultrasound scans on most pregnant women in the west these days to check for abnormalities in the foetus? Will I conclude that this is a 'good thing', as giving birth to an abnormal baby, with all the extra time for caring that would involve, would jeopardise my chances of becoming a senior partner in the law firm in which I work? Or, if I am feminist inspired by the passion of radical feminist rhetoric on the perils of patriarchy, what will I think about 'test-tube babies'? Unlike my 'liberal sister', I am not likely to think that as this provides more choice for women this is automatically a 'good thing'. Instead I am more likely to consider this as another example of patriarchal control over women's bodies and spend time documenting what women suffer in order to conceive a baby through in vitro fertilisation (IVF). Already we can see that different theories can lead to different stories and beliefs about practices. This matters.

A second reason why this is a good area of practice to select is that questions about the practices of reproductive technologies imply questions about women. This is very good for our purposes here because one of the key areas of division between modernist and postmodernist feminists clusters around the question of woman and women. Those feminists who favour more traditional or modernist approaches feel very unhappy about the (seeming) postmodern abandonment of the category of woman as the indisputable starting point for feminist theory and politics. If postmodern feminism cannot speak about women, as more traditional feminists might argue, how can this help women to think about and deal with a practical issue such as ultra-sound screening? This question about using the category of woman has been discussed at length in theory but what does it actually mean in practice? These are the kinds of questions I shall address in this book.

In the rest of this chapter I shall introduce some of the key themes and ideas from the four large categories of feminist thought I am starting with – liberal, radical, socialist and postmodern. In Chapter 2 I shall identify the key themes that will enable me to evaluate the idea that there is a gulf between 1970s modernist feminisms and 1990s postmodern feminisms; namely the subject, epistemology and politics. In Chapter 3 I shall discuss modernist feminisms through the practices of reproductive technologies and do the same for postmodern feminisms in Chapter 4. Chapter 5 will return to the question of the gulf between feminist theories and serve as an overall conclusion to the book.

## Liberal feminism

As a way to start thinking about some of the central characteristics of liberal feminism, I want to introduce six words or concepts: *freedom, choice, rights, equality, rationality* and *control*. None of these six concepts typically associated with liberal feminism sounds very subversive or unreasonable in the context of contemporary liberal democracies, such as the United Kingdom or the United States. Intuitively we might think that of course we want and should be entitled to be free, to have choices and rights, to be treated equally, and to be able to exercise rationality and have control over our lives. In a very real sense, these things are the essence of liberal democracy. However, I think it still comes as a bit of a shock to realise that only as recently as the 1960s, women in the UK were not paid the same income as men for doing exactly the same job. This is one small but powerful reminder that women have traditionally been treated rather differently to men, and this has had all kinds of effects on women's lives. Two of the main goals of liberal feminism have been to expose old-fashioned ideas about what women are and should do, and to allow, even encourage, women to do the same things as men for the same status and rewards.

An early example of arguments made on these lines appears in Mary Wollstonecraft's *A Vindication of the Rights of Woman*, first published in 1792. Wollstonecraft was deeply distressed at the way women were essentially trained to be weak and pathetic creatures. She described them as 'the feathered race', like birds confined to cages who have nothing to do but plume themselves and 'stalk with mock majesty from perch to perch' (Wollstonecraft, 1988: 55). Her passionate cry for JUSTICE (which she writes in capitals herself) for women (one half of the human race) was inspired both by her observation of women in society but also in response to one of the major political theorists at the time (and still very influential), Jean-Jacques Rousseau. Wollstonecraft's anger was not surprising given some of the ideas he had. For example, in *Émile* (first published in 1762), Rousseau claimed that

> the education of women should always be relative to men. To please, to be useful to us, to make us love and esteem them, to educate us when young, and take care of us when grown up, to advise us, to console us, to render our lives easy and agreeable: these are the duties of women at all times, and what they should be taught in their infancy.
>
> (Rousseau 1955: 328)

Wollstonecraft simply could not agree with this, and was impelled to argue against it, using some of the contemporary arguments from her time, primarily ones based on *natural rights*. She, like many of the writers that influenced her (including Thomas Paine and John Locke), believed that individuals had natural rights and that all men were equal to each other. The main thing that differentiated men from animals was man's rationality. Wollstonecraft simply extended these arguments to include women, and this practice of 'including women in' is something liberal feminists have done ever since.

In the eighteenth century, Mary Wollstonecraft argued that girls should have the same education as boys. In France around the same time, Olympe de Gouges insisted on the extension of the egalitarian principles of the French Declaration of the Rights of Man to women. In the nineteenth century, Elizabeth Cady Stanton in the United States drew up a document called the 'Declaration of Sentiments', based on the Declaration of Independence, claiming that both men and women were equal (Donovan, 1988: 5). Back in Britain John Stuart Mill and Harriet Taylor Mill were writing radical books suggesting that women be granted all political privileges, including the right to vote and the right to run for public office (Mill, 1970; Taylor, 1970).

### Why can't a woman be more like a man?

Being treated like men and being allowed to do what men do is a consistent theme within liberal feminist thought. In the twentieth century this has resulted in demands for equal pay, equal rights to employment opportunities and a right to be part of the public world of politics and paid work – just like men. The strategies to achieve this have included using legislation, for example in the United Kingdom the Equal Pay Act in 1970 and the Sex Discrimination Act in 1975. The idea that women are discriminated against because of their sex has led to a number of strategies to combat this. Echoing Wollstonecraft's earlier claim that women were trained to be pathetic, many twentieth-century liberal feminists argued that 'gender role stereotyping' was responsible for training women to be less successful than men. Liberal feminists suggested that girls should stop being brought up to be passive and lacking in confidence and instead encouraged to develop into assertive independent human beings. Similarly, employers and educators should resist the traditional tendency to channel girls into 'typically female' (and usually low-paid) jobs such as nursing or secretarial work. In the 1960s and 1970s liberal feminists shaped many of the major political programmes in the United States Women's Movement. Betty Friedan founded the National Organisation for Women (NOW) in 1966. This group campaigned for equal civil rights, equal access to education, health and welfare and equal pay for women. Some liberal feminists made the case for the introduction of positive or reverse discrimination (alternatively known as 'affirmative action', especially in the United States). This would be an intermediate step to reverse the effects of the long-standing discrimination against women. For example, in applications for jobs, reverse discrimination would imply that the job be given to a female candidate, all other things being equal (Hawkesworth, 1990: 171–197; Humm, 1992: 181).

### Getting rid of gender?

A just future would be one without gender. In its social structures and practices, one's sex would have no more relevance than one's eye color or the length of one's toes.

(Okin, 1989: 171)

Why would anyone want a genderless world? For the principles of justice, equality, freedom and rights, to name a few reasons. Liberal feminists have consistently claimed that women have not been granted these freedoms and rights because of their sex. This has resulted in a harder life for women often because of restricted access to money and status. All kinds of arguments have been used to justify these sex-based restrictions. In the nineteenth century the basis for such justifications was frequently made in the realm of the physiological. For example, in 1874 the Chair of Harvard Medical School published a book (*Sex in Education: A Fair Chance for the Girls*) in which he claimed that educating girls to the same standard as boys ran the risk of making women sterile, as women would pay too much attention to the development of their brains rather than to their menstrual functions! (Hubbard, 1990: 39). On the other side of the Atlantic, the president of the British Medical Association in 1886 argued that educating women might prevent women from giving birth to sons.

And the human race will have lost those who should have been her sons . . . Bacon, for want of a mother, will not be born . . . Women are made and meant to be, not men, but mothers of men.

(Quoted in Hubbard, 1990: 39)

Justifications for differential treatment of the sexes in the realm of the emotional and psychological have also regularly been used. In fact, the concept of 'typical female behaviour' has, over the last couple of centuries, often been associated with irrationality, even madness (Ussher, 1991). It is interesting to remember, however, that women's madness is often directly linked back to their physiology. The genesis of the word describing the operation to remove a woman's womb – *hysterectomy* – refers to the removal of the 'root' of women's hysteria.

These justifications seem absurd in western liberal democracies as we move into the twenty-first century. Laughable even. The physiological justifications in the nineteenth century extended to the 'bigger is better' argument, implying that as women's brains are generally smaller than men's, this meant that men were intellectually superior to women. But researchers keen to prove this point ran into a problem when they realised that this logically implied elephants and whales were intellectually superior to men (Saunders and Platt, 1997: 177)! What liberal feminists wanted to do is show how mistaken these justifications and arguments were.

### Reactions and results

In this new century it will be tempting to think that all those bizarre explanations for treating women differently to men have been completely eradicated, particularly in the western world. Maybe they have. But it is instructive to remember the reactions to those who campaigned for women's rights and freedoms in the context of liberal ideals. Mary Wollstonecraft, for example, was labelled as suffering from 'penis envy'. And those women who campaigned for the vote for women in the late nineteenth and early twentieth century were frequently represented as ugly old spinsters. A cartoon published in 1870 showed five suffragettes who basically looked like sour, grumpy, ugly old women. The caption to the cartoon suggested that these women had 'never been kissed'. The poem that went along with the cartoon carried on with the image that women who demand 'too much' are perhaps lacking in particular areas!

> The rights of Women who demand,
> Those women are but few:
> The greater part had rather stand
> Exactly as they do.
>
> Beauty has claims, for which she fights
> At ease, with winning arms;

> The women who want women's rights
> Want, mostly, Woman's charms.
>
> (Hassal, J. quoted in Atkinson, 1997: 8)

In the United Kingdom women over 21 years of age were granted the vote in 1928. As I write this in 1999, there has been a female British prime minister and there are 101 women members of parliament. In the majority of western countries discrimination on the grounds of sex is illegal. It would seem that liberal feminists have been resoundingly successful.

## Radical feminism

Radical feminists are the ones the media love to hate. These are the feminists who are frequently represented as the 'feminazis' or the 'politically correct Stalinist feminists'. These representations have largely been responsible for the construction of a caricature of 'a radical feminist', who is more often than not a fat, ugly woman with short hair and bad dress sense. Typically, there is an assumption of lesbianism too. When asked what she thought of the word 'feminist', a recently elected woman member of parliament in the British Labour government gave this response.

> What is a feminist? I am in that I believe I'm equal and valued on my ability rather than my gender. But I don't see myself as the hairy-legged dyke stereotype. I fought for equal pay, but I still look like a woman.
>
> (Fitzsimons, 1997: 75)

This response has an edge of anxiety to it. Lorna Fitzsimons seems very keen not to be associated with anything too radical, here represented partially by 'excess' body hair! A radical feminist might claim that Lorna Fitzsimons has a slight disgust for women who do not conform to western standards of femininity (heterosexual and hairy only in the 'right' places). Perhaps the 'loathing and disgust' for things female, as referred to in Germaine Greer's influential book *The Female Eunuch* (1970) has some contemporary relevance.

Let me introduce six central features or concepts associated with radical feminism: *woman centred*, *patriarchy*, *oppression*, *experience*, *control* and *'the personal is political'*. These six features have a rather different feel to them than the liberal feminist concepts, although one is superficially the same, namely *control*. Some of the ideas and beliefs suggested by these concepts do appear to be somewhat old-fashioned, even unreasonable in western democracies in the early 2000s. Take, for example, this statement from the manifesto of the New York Red-stockings (a group of radical feminists) written in 1969.

> Women are an oppressed class. Our oppression is total, affecting every facet of our lives. We are exploited as objects, breeders, domestic servants and cheap labor. We are considered inferior beings whose only purpose is to enhance men's lives . . . *All men* have oppressed women.
>
> (Quoted in Bryson, 1992: 183–184, emphasis in original)

Or this quote from Mary Daly: 'Patriarchy is itself the prevailing religion of the entire planet' (1979: 39). These bold, assertive and universalist claims at first glance do seem inappropriate, at least in a western environment in this new century. Entering parliament as a new member, Lorna Fitzsimons is perhaps understandably reluctant to want to believe that 'her oppression is total', or that her sex makes her useful only to 'enhance men's lives'. Could she do her job properly if she believed that 'all men oppress all women?'

### Man-haters?

But it is true that men are a problem for radical feminists – such a problem for one writer, Valerie Solanas (1968), that she created the *Society for Cutting Up Men* (SCUM). One key way in which men are seen as a problem by radical feminists is that they always seem to be at the centre of things and controlling them – things that matter anyway. Men still have the top jobs, the most money, the most land, the most privileges. Of course, liberal feminists noticed this too, but they tended to think that this was largely the result of old-fashioned and misogynist ideas which could be rectified with time and reason. Radical feminists had a hard time agreeing with this because they suspected that more was at work than simple mistakes or even misogyny. What was at work was patriarchy.

The introduction of the concept of patriarchy has had an enormous impact. One simple definition of patriarchy is male domination but this does not simply mean the domination of individual men or groups of men over women but *structural* domination. One way to think about the concept of structure is as a system of hierarchical values embedded in society. And within patriarchal society this simply – but with huge implications – means that what gets associated with men and masculinity is generally given a higher value than things associated with women and femininity. This idea of a patriarchal structure is very important as it gives radical feminists a way of explaining why women are so consistently disadvantaged compared to men.

> The concept and theory of patriarchy is essential to capture the depth, pervasiveness and interconnectedness of different aspects of women's subordination, and can be developed in such a way as to take account of the different forms of gender inequality over time, class and ethnic group.
>
> (Walby, 1990: 2)

The structural theory of patriarchy suggested that it wasn't simply men who were the problem but all things associated with men and masculinity. This meant that not only did men dominate – but so did masculine values, ideas and typical modes of living. This basically covered everything, including such things as the mind, knowledge and emotions. Or science. Or technology. Or literature. Or personal lives. Anything and everything. It's not just that men were largely responsible for producing scientific knowledge or machines (although they were). The more significant point was that men and the values and priorities of masculinity were responsible for deciding and controlling what *counted* as scientific knowledge, or anything else. Radical feminists decided to turn that upside-down and place women at the centre.

### Women first

What might happen if women were at the centre? What would the world look like? Finding an answer to this is not so easy. It's not so obvious that if Britain had 600 women MPs, that parliament or the country would run any differently. But radical feminists were more interested in focusing on what women usually did, rather than what men usually did. What if what women did *traditionally* were put at the centre and considered to be of great importance? Six-figure salaries for mothers perhaps? And it wasn't just what women usually did that radical feminists wanted to place as central, but how women traditionally *thought*.

This might seem bizarre and it is not unproblematic. But think about it. If for centuries men have dominated much of what counted as important – countries, political analyses, religion, to name a few things – and one result of that was that women were disadvantaged, it must surely have something to do with that domination? And this did not simply extend to judgements about the value of the different things that women did to men. It also extended to what were superficially the *same* things. We have all seen the popular poster on office walls which captures this sense of 'same but different'. Some examples would include, '*he* gets on well with his colleagues/*she* is always gossiping', '*he* is having lunch with the boss – *he* must be in for a promotion/*she* must be having an affair', '*she's* late for work – *she* must be shopping/*he* must be in a meeting'.

A radical feminist might turn to a liberal feminist and say that it doesn't matter if women learn to do the same things as men, they won't be treated or understood in the same way. The cartoon that depicts five men and one woman sitting round a table in a meeting and one of the men is saying something like 'that's an excellent suggestion Miss Jones, perhaps one of the men here would like to make it', captures another aspect of this patriarchal hierarchy of value. It suggests that things are only given real value when 'maleness' is attached to them in some way.

### New realities

Radical feminism is typically associated with depressing stories about male violence and female victimisation which have led to its description as 'victim feminism'. But this idea of a being a victim is at odds with the exhilaration that countless women must have experienced who were released from debilitating beliefs about themselves because of radical feminism's re-descriptions of their experiences. Women who got angry with their children no longer had to regard themselves as simply 'bad mothers'. Who wouldn't get frustrated being cooped up in a house all day with a small child? What a revelation it must have been for those women who were beaten by their husbands for not having the dinner on the table to realise that this was a totally unacceptable violent act. Radical feminism re-describes reality. This means that something that was previously thought of as 'not violent', now can be re-described as (domestic) violence. This has enormous consequences for women's lives. Indeed, it must have encouraged many women to stop being victims.

How were radical feminists to start thinking about all that patriarchal knowledge that had been constructed over the centuries and passed down as 'truth'? Not by using the same methods as men, that's for sure. Radical feminists opened up ways of thinking to include all sorts of things and methods previously disregarded as irrelevant. Using women's experiences and own versions of the truth for example.

> [Radical feminist knowledge] is created directly from the experi-
> ence of women, and it reflects women's pain and anger. It does
> not arbitrarily limit its sources of information, but utilizes women's
> special ways of knowing. Its non-linear mode of expression reflects
> the human learning process, and the highly charged language of its
> authors evokes an emotional response in its readers and helps jolt
> their consciousness out of the conceptual frameworks of patriarchy
> and into a woman-centred paradigm.
>
> (Jaggar, 1983: 369)

Take a look at scientific knowledge. One radical feminist scholar, trained as a scientist, posed this question: 'How much of the nature of science is bound up with the idea of masculinity, and what would it mean for science if it were otherwise?' (Keller, 1985: 3). Radical feminists scrutinised scientific texts for evidence of ideas associated with masculinity and came up with plenty of examples. Here is one from Francis Bacon. If you recall from the previous section, Bacon is one of the 'sons' that might not have been born if women got 'over-educated' and ended up with withered ovaries according to a British medical expert.

> For you have but to hound nature in her wanderings and you will
> be able when you like to lead and drive her afterwards to the same
> place again. Neither ought a man to make scruple of entering and
> penetrating into those holes and corners when the inquisition of
> truth is his whole object.
>
> (Quoted in Harding, 1991: 43)

Feminist scientists argued that scientific theory and practice was saturated with such masculinist imagery, and in this particular example heterosexual imagery. This is significant for radical feminists because they claim that the effect is to reinforce general ideas about the 'natural' inferiority and passivity of women who needed controlling.

### Fear and loathing

Radical feminism is susceptible to being presented in ways that make it easy to dismiss it as outdated and over the top. There has been a tendency, amongst feminists and non-feminists alike, to look back to the early texts and search out the most outrageous and dogmatic statements and use them as evidence of radical feminism's contemporary uselessness. Perhaps it is the sense of fear, loathing and disgust that radical feminists bring to the surface that makes people uncomfortable. Perhaps a radical feminist's description of fear is too much for many people. One example in the context of reproductive technologies is:

> Sitting at my typewriter at night, I see my writing on the new reproductive technologies as a scream of warning to other women.
>
> (Corea, quoted in Barr, 1988: 171)

Other examples regarding men's violence and supposed hatred of women include:

> Male aggression is rapacious. It spills over, not accidentally, but purposefully. There is war. Older men create wars . . . Older men hate boys because boys have the smell of women on them. War purifies, washes off the female stink.
>
> (Dworkin, 1989: 51)

> Women have very little idea of how much men hate them.
>
> (Greer, 1970: 249)

Not many laughs here. It all feels *very* uncomfortable and people generally prefer to feel comfortable. Together with radical feminists' desire fully to document the violence done towards women, especially in the arenas of sexuality and reproduction – some of the most private and intimate spheres of life – perhaps it is not surprising that many have wanted to evade, ignore or dismiss radical feminist arguments.

Because of this it is important to mention that radical feminism can be considered as having scored some remarkable successes. Simply giving women 'permission' to put their lives and experiences at the centre is surely an unprecedented event in the history of social and political theory. Furthermore the altered version of reality that comes along with that can be regarded as a significant achievement. The exposing of a hierarchy of values which, more often than not, placed activities associated with men at the top and those associated with women at the bottom is a most radical revelation. And the realisation that this gendered hierarchy works its way into hugely important influences on people's lives, from science and technology at one end of the scale, to the family and one's own sense of self at the other end, is a profound one. For radical feminists believed that every aspect of one's life was subject to the constraints of patriarchy – not just in the public world. One result of their insistence of placing women's lives and experiences at the centre was to argue that 'the personal is political'. This meant that all activities and experiences should be politically scrutinised – including the most intimate ones. It's not that radical feminists *made* the private realm political – they exposed how it already always is political. Does this all imply radical feminism is now useless?

## Socialist feminism

Some lines from a poem entitled *The Socialist and the Suffragist* by Charlotte Perkins Gilman nicely introduce one of the traditional arguments between socialism and feminism – that is one between class and gender.[2]

> 'A lifted world lifts women up'
> The Socialist explained.
> 'You cannot lift the world at all
> While half of it is kept so small,'
> The Suffragist maintained.
>
> The world awoke and tartly spoke:
> 'Your work is all the same;
> Work together or work apart,
> Work, each of you, with all your heart
> Just get into the game.'

> (Reprinted in Hansen and Philipson, 1990: v)

### Class or gender?

> What's a socialist feminist? Someone who goes to twice as many meetings.
>
> (1970s joke)

The lines from the poem above suggest that there is an argument going on between a socialist and a suffragist. The former is obviously more interested in the inequalities brought about by class oppression, whereas the latter is more concerned with discrimination against women. In contemporary language this can be summed up as the tension between class and gender. Questions raised by this include: Is one more important than the other? Are class and gender inevitably intertwined? Socialist feminists have spent much time thinking about such issues, leading to the development of a rich body of feminist thought and practice. Let me introduce six of the central features of socialist feminism: *class/capitalism*, *revolution*, *patriarchy*, *psychoanalysis*, *subjectivity* and *difference*. These six features suggest a wide-ranging and eclectic mixture of ideas and influences which minimally include Marxism, radical feminism and psychoanalysis. This mixture of influences together with the tensions over class versus gender all combine to make socialist feminism a fascinating and very complex set of ideas and practices. Additionally, the fortunes of the politics of socialism around the world over the last couple of decades (especially with the demise of the Soviet Union) have necessarily impacted on all forms of theoretical socialism, including socialist feminism. This all adds to the complexity of contemporary socialist feminism.

### Marxist or socialist feminism?

Clearly socialist feminism has been deeply influenced by Marxism but I think the term 'socialist feminism' more accurately captures the breadth and numerous strands of this form of feminism. Nevertheless, it was Marxist theories of class and capitalism that initially inspired socialist feminists. However, their concern with women's specific experiences within capitalism led them in a variety of directions. Initially a classic argument was that women were second-class citizens within systems of capitalism and patriarchy. Such systems depended on the exploitation of working people and the special exploitation of women (Humm, 1989: 213). Marxist principles were applied to analyse how women's work in the home was crucial to the functioning of capitalism and yet how it was not regarded as 'real work' as it was not part of the market economy. This application of Marxist ideas about work and radical feminist ideas about patriarchy and the political nature of the private realm led to the development of two parallel debates: the domestic labour debate and the dual systems versus unified systems debate.

### Patriarchy or capitalism? Patriarchy and capitalism?

If a revolution were to happen – and Marxists and socialists have traditionally demanded a revolutionary overthrow of capitalism – then the theory has to be right, which for early socialist feminists implied that the causes of oppression and exploitation had to be identified. Using Marxist principles alone was not sufficient as these did not take women's experiences seriously enough. Radical feminist views about patriarchy were also found to be wanting as they tended to assume too universalistic and static a view of patriarchy and women's oppression. What was required was a more overarching and complete theory of oppression. Those favouring dual-systems theory argued that the systems of patriarchy and capitalism were distinct but intersected. Unified systems theorists claimed that the two systems could not be separated. This debate and the domestic labour debate went on for a rather long time – one practical suggestion arising was that there should be wages for housework. This is still not a suggestion that any government seems to take seriously, despite the realisation that housewives do indeed do a lot of work!

### *Still not enough . . .*

Despite long debates mainly in the pages of academic journals, Marxism and radical feminism proved not to be enough for socialist feminists, so they turned to psychoanalytic theory for help. An early influential article was Juliet Mitchell's, 'Women: The Longest Revolution' (1966). This was perhaps a surprising move at the time as feminists had heavily criticised psychoanalytic theory for its sexism and misogyny. As one recent writer described it,

> Mary Daly gleefully demonstrates that the word 'therapist' can be read as 'the/rapist' and that Andrea Dworkin calls Freud a pornographer in 'real life' and in Freudian theory men use the penis to deliver death to women who are, literally, in their genitals, dirt to the men.
>
> (Gardiner, 1992: 438)

However, Mitchell's article and subsequent book (1974) alerted feminists to the need for a capitalist *and* psychic revolution. Feminists could use psychoanalytic theories to explore and expose the construction of *gendered* identities or subjectivities with a view to working out how to achieve a change in the negative aspects of such constructions. If psychoanalysis taught us that 'biology was not destiny', and instead revealed some of the processes through which the human social being emerges from the biological being, then this surely implied the tools of psychoanalysis could now be used to construct a picture of how women's subjectivities were created. If it could be shown that women's particular 'feminine ways of being' were a social and cultural construction and not a biological inevitability, then they could be altered, which would help erase sexism and male domination.

### Different subjectivities = different knowledges?

Ideas about 'differently gendered subjectivities' paved the way for some feminists to argue that women reasoned and thought differently to men. Of course, traditionally this gendered difference has been considered inferior. Some feminists, however, were keen not to deny the difference but to acknowledge and use it. In the area of moral reasoning, for example, a particularly influential and contested book suggested that women and girls 'failed' on traditional scales of moral reasoning because such scales were based on boys and men (Gilligan, 1982). It was not Gilligan's intention to try and persuade others that women had the same moral reasoning power as men, rather she wanted to pursue the idea that women had a *different* way of reasoning morally.

Other feminists traced the causes of gendered differences. Nancy Chodorow, for example, argued that girls gradually became 'engendered' from a very early age, and as a result developed the desire to 'mother' and to be 'feminine' from early on (1978). These were not roles that girls chose, instead they impinged themselves deep into the psyche. Chodorow's analysis drew heavily from the Oedipus conflict – an infamous psychoanalytic concept – as she believed that girls and boys resolved this conflict differently, in part because of their different bodily relationship to the mother. Boys had metaphorically to tear themselves away from their relationship with the mother, which resulted in a personality that was more autonomous and separate, and so unsuitable for the mothering role. Girls, on the other hand, identified with the mother and had no need to go through a painful separation process as they grew up, with the result that girls could 'relate' to other people more and this made them more suitable for the mothering role.

This kind of analysis about differently gendered subjectivites led many feminists towards building up a whole new theory based on the Marxist notion that the theory has to be 'right' in order that desired practical outcomes can be achieved. This theory known as feminist *standpoint theory* implied that differently gendered subjectivities lead to different knowledges. This might be thought of as the special contribution of socialist feminism which 'was to begin the construction of a new theoretical framework that would show the quality and systematic interrelations of familiar features of women's contemporary oppression' (Jaggar, 1983: 316–317). This will be discussed further in the next chapter.

## More complexities about difference

Given socialist feminists' commitment to analysing class as well as gender, it's not surprising that other forms of difference began to be impossible to ignore. Ignoring differences around race and sexuality was a major criticism levelled at socialist feminists. In 1984 a group of black feminists took over editorial control of the socialist feminist journal *Feminist Review*, in which the claim was made that 'a particular tradition, white, Eurocentric and Western, has sought to establish itself as the only legitimate feminism in current political practice' (Amos and Parmar, 1984: 3).

> Socialist feminists have had to deal seriously with charges of racism and Western bias in their construction of theories which are predicated on the relationship between class and gender hierarchies, to the outright neglect, or at best, the marginalization, of other axes of oppression.
>
> (Marshall, 1994: 86)

The issue of sexuality too, much of it stemming from radical feminism, caused major problems for socialist feminism. For some feminists, it was the issue of sexuality, rather than race, which produced the fundamental rift between feminists at the end of the 1970s and which 'shattered any potential unity about the nature, direction and goal of feminism' (Segal, 1987: 65). Briefly put, the existence of lesbianism and the concomitant issues of political lesbianism and/or separatism combined with the radical feminist insistence on the reality of men's violence added further tension and complexity to socialist feminist theory and practice.

A flavour of that complexity can be found in this list of socialist feminist aims outlined by Alison Jaggar in 1983, namely: to reconstruct knowledge (Jaggar, 1983: 377); to abolish class and gender (ibid.: 317); to better material conditions (ibid.: 318); to abolish workerhood and womanhood as social categories (ibid.: 343); to construct a political economy of women's subordination (ibid.: 134); and the material overthrow of male domination (ibid.: 384). All this was to be achieved by material and psychic revolution. A liberal feminist in the 1990s might turn to a socialist feminist and remark on the lack of success in achieving all these aims!

### Contemporary decline?

In many ways, socialist feminism can be seen as a particularly reflective and responsive form of feminism, which is perhaps in part responsible for its contemporary complexity. Additionally, with socialist politics world-wide going out of fashion, those who had called themselves socialist feminists have had to ask searching questions about the usefulness of the label in the late 1990s. In a Reader on Socialist Feminism, four writers discussed the questions: 'Where is socialist feminism today? Has it died, and if so, why has it died?' (Hansen and Philipson, 1990: 301). One view was that socialist feminism had died because it had been 'narrowed and hobbled by academic environs; it's been shaped to the demands of academia and it's been cut off from any kind of movement' (ibid.: 310). Another view was that what socialist feminists had tried to do was worthwhile.

> We had to understand the entire structure of society not just personal relations, not just things like male violence, the way other feminists were doing. We really were trying to get to the roots, like radicals, and Marxism seemed like the best set of tools available for doing that job. I think we were right to pick up those tools and use them, and I don't think the tools were wrong either; I think sometimes we misused them.
>
> (Ibid.: 313–314)

Another suggestion was that what was needed was to hold on to the idea that feminism is big enough to include everything in its perspective, was 'a non-1960s politics that still can talk about the realities of class, that has an international view of women's fate, that can take on the really deep questions about the future of humanity' (ibid.: 315). A large set of very ambitious aims!

### But there's still class . . .

Socialist feminism in the early 2000s is something of an enigma. In the United States there has been a tendency to conflate socialist feminism with radical feminism. And the contemporary discomfort with the word 'socialist' makes it difficult to retain any sense that it could possibly be relevant today. I think it is important to resist the tendency to make hasty dismissals or judgements. As with radical feminism, it seems bizarre to dismiss the successes of socialist feminism. For example, highlighting how women suffer disproportionately to men because of the demands of capitalism and the profit motive has been of vital significance. And like all feminisms, socialist feminism is important as a source of analysis and criticism of other feminisms – keeping other feminisms more 'honest'. And many would claim that 'class stratification is alive and well, as is the racial discrimination with which economic disparities are so regularly entwined' (Chancer, 1998: 26). If this is accurate, can it be true that socialist feminism is now (virtually) useless?

## Postmodern feminism

> What do you get if you cross a postmodernist with a member of the Mafia? An offer you can't understand.
>
> (1990s joke)

Postmodernism has a reputation for being inaccessible and very difficult to understand – as the joke suggests. Whether this is a fair or significant assessment and whether it applies to postmodern feminism as well are moot points. Despite the alleged inaccessibility, it is still possible to select some central features of this form of feminism. For example: *the subject, language,* power/truth/knowledge, *anti-metanarrative, anti-foundational* and *deconstruction*. These features could equally well apply to postmodernism on its own, thus begging the question, 'Where and what is the feminism in postmodern feminism?' Let me start addressing that question by stating that postmodern feminism emerges from two main sources. First, out of criticisms of modernist feminist theorising and second, perhaps obviously, from postmodern and poststructural thought.[3] Following from this, postmodern feminists are especially keen to expose the flaws and weaknesses of traditional feminisms, particularly in regard to their modernist commitments. One of the significant areas in which this takes place is through the destabilisation of the category of woman. Let us take a look at how this works.

### *And ain't I a woman?*

> I have plowed and planted and gathered into barns and no man could head me! And ain't I a woman? I could work as much and eat as much as a man – when I could get it – and bear the lash as well! And ain't I a woman? I have borne thirteen children and

seen most all sold off to slavery, and when I cried out with my
mother's grief, none but Jesus heard me. And ain't I a woman?
(Sojourner Truth, Women's Convention in Akron, Ohio, 1851)

This evocative plea by black abolitionist and freed slave Sojourner
Truth was made in order to deny that she was defined by her frailty –
a typical feminine virtue or attribute for genteel (white, middle-class)
women in the nineteenth century. But Sojourner Truth's words also
show that she wanted to claim some 'femininity' – or femaleness –
that she was a mother and overwhelmed with maternal grief when
her children were taken away from her. In many ways she was like a
man *and* a woman. Though if the man who had previously owned
her as a slave had been asked whether she was a man or a woman,
clearly the answer would have been that Sojourner Truth was a
woman. Her reproductive capacities alone surely proved this. But he
would also have treated her as if she were a man, expecting her to
work and be punished in the same way as (black/slave) men. At the
same time the owner would probably have found it inconceivable to
imagine Sojourner Truth on the same planet at his wife or daughter.
So what does it really mean to say one is a man or a woman?

Modernist feminists have been pretty clear about the answer to this
question. For example, modernist feminists typically draw upon ideas
about the human subject which developed from the age of the Enlightenment. The well-known phrase from René Descartes – 'I think therefore I am' – serves as a good example of Enlightenment thinking about
the human subject or 'the self'. At first glance Descartes' words might
not seem particularly insightful. But they really do indicate a stark
and profound move away from beliefs in supreme authorities, such
as god or the king, as the ultimately most significant producer of
truth and knowledge. With the age of the Enlightenment dawned the
very new idea that it was human individuals (the 'I') who were the
proper and ultimate producers of knowledge and truth. This move
from a kind of 'slave owner mentality' towards the primacy and dignity
of the human subject formed the basis for a whole host of claims for
rights and self-definition with which we are so familiar today.

Postmodernist feminists have not wanted to be drawn into the same
ways of thinking. They claim that the existence of a such an 'ultimate'
subject, whether god or man, is an illusion. If modernists think of the
human subject like an apple, with a vital core, then postmodernists
think of the subject more like an onion – peel away the layers and
there is nothing there at the end or at the core. This doesn't mean
that human subjects (people) don't exist or are not important. It is to

do with questions about what forms human subjects and what constitutes the basis of them. For modernists there is an ultimate core to the
self or the subject which inspires modernist feminists to 'tell it like it is'
about woman, in other words to say what woman is and should be.
Postmodernist feminists, on the other hand, claim that there is no
vital core and thus prefer to ask 'How do women become or get said?'

### An identity all of my own. What more could a girl want?

Postmodernist feminists also claim that fixing the identity of woman is
not a good idea. For these feminists, the last thing a 'girl' should want is
to be tied to an identity, whatever it is (Elam, 1994: 71). In many ways
postmodern feminists don't care what that identity is. It could be a
'rational human' or an 'earth mother' or 'a worker'. It is the practice,
process and effects (how women 'get said') of attempting to make an
identity stick that bothers postmodern feminists. They claim that any
attempt to make an identity stick is *always* an authoritarian practice.
For example, Rousseau's identification of women as 'men's little help-
mates' and Wollstonecraft's identification of women as essentially or
potentially 'just as good as men' can both be counted as authoritarian
practices as their aim is to define and decide what woman is or what
women are capable of. Of course, a radical feminist might say one
definition is better than the other. But for postmodernist feminists,
this is not the point they are most concerned with.

   The debate about what woman is 'supposed to be' and attempts to
settle the question are not new, within feminism or social and political
theory and philosophy generally. Both Plato and Aristotle raised the
'question of woman'. Plato included women as members of the
guardian class while Aristotle decided woman was a 'nourishing
medium' for man's sperm (Feder *et al.*, 1997: 1). One can go through
a whole host of eminent thinkers – Kant, Rousseau, Hegel, Nietzsche,
Freud, Lacan, Derrida – and find that they had or have a position on
the question of woman (what she is supposed to be or do, or what
counts as a good or bad woman). And it is not only men that have
defined women (for good or bad), women do it all the time. A recent
example is the statement made by Ann Widdecombe, a British
member of parliament, commenting on the wives of the leaders of the
two main political parties: 'Ffion is a proper wife, she keeps out of
the limelight, not like Cherie Blair' (*Independent on Sunday*, 25 October
1998).[4] This is clearly an example of someone deciding, even 'knowing'
what the proper role of a woman in the position of 'leader's wife'
should be. Ann Widdecombe is not herself married and her views

appear to be 'feminist unfriendly'. But many self-defined (modernist) feminists have consistently also defined what woman is, should be or might be. As one feminist puts it, '[modernist] feminist theory is engaged in redefining Woman' (Grant, 1993: 127).

### Only words?

One of the important ways in which we define things is through the medium of language. And for postmodernists, definitions through language are not simply about naming, it is about the construction of meaning and subjectivity. Thought and meaning are constructed through language and there can be no meaning outside language. It is the place where our sense of ourselves and where our subjectivity is constructed (Weedon, 1987: 21). Another crucial point to understand is that meaning is *itself* arbitrary and unfixed and only given form by reference to other meanings (Jackson, 1992: 26). Or as one writer phrases it, 'meaning is constructed through the counterposition of differing elements whose definition lies precisely in their difference from each other' (Barrett, 1992: 202). So for example, 'western' is understood in opposition to 'eastern', 'north' to 'south', 'man' to 'woman' and 'good' to 'bad'.

Many postmodernists, feminist and otherwise, have been very influenced in this area by the work on structural linguistics of Ferdinand de Saussure (1974). Language for Saussure does not just reflect an already existing social reality but constitutes that reality for us. Different languages divide up social reality in different ways, and so construct different meanings. Thus simple translations from one language to another cannot hope to be true or accurate representations (Barrett, 1992: 203; Weedon, 1987: 22). For example, meanings of masculinity and femininity will change between different languages, cultures, and historical periods. Trying to tie the meaning down is to give at best a false impression and at worst another example of the closure and the power which postmodernists attempt to expose.

### Power/truth/knowledge

Linked to the idea that all meanings are arbitrary and that subjects are constructed, feminist postmodernists claim that a 'one truth' or undisputed knowledge does not exist and logically, therefore, the human 'knowing subject' cannot be the ultimate source of it. If the Cartesian self (from René Descartes' 'I think therefore I am') is an illusion, then it cannot ground knowledge and justice in the way that modernists think it can (Coole, 1993: 195). Many postmodern writers do not just say that there is no such thing as truth or knowledge, they also argue that what has masqueraded as truth is largely an exercise of power. Foucault, for example, was not interested in examining which truth claims were false (as typifies modernist projects) but in understanding why and how certain beliefs get to be considered truth. For Foucault, those who define truth possess power.

We can see therefore that those who define woman – whoever they are – are playing a power game. The feminist postmodern move away from modernist certainties about the category of woman, for example, has implied an emphasis on gender as a source of power and hierarchy. Indeed, power has become a major category in this analysis.

> Truth isn't outside power, or lacking in power . . . truth is a thing of this world: it is produced only by virtue of multiple forms of constraint. And it induces regular effects of power. Each society has its regime of truth . . . the types of discourse which it accepts and makes function as true; the mechanisms and instances which enable one to distinguish true and false statements.
>
> (Grant, 1993: 131)

A postmodern feminist task is not then to find out what woman is, but to expose the power/truth/knowledge game that goes on in defining what woman is. The use of the word 'game' is not intended to minimise the seriousness of such a task.

### Anti-everything?

It is certainly the case that postmodernists are keen to develop ideas about the social world that do not rely on traditional understandings (Fraser and Nicholson, 1990: 21). Grand and overarching theories (sometimes called *meta-narratives*) which appear to try and explain the whole of social reality, are a chief target of attack. These totalising theories which purport to be universal are seen by postmodernists as an unwelcome hangover from the Enlightenment–humanist quest for total explanation, prediction and control. One example of such a theory is Marxism – but of course feminism is another. The field of social reality is seen by postmodernists to be far too complex and heterogeneous to be understood by utilising sweeping generalisations and all-encompassing theories. To explain the lives of massive groups of people by reference to general categories such as race, gender or class is too reductive.

Contemporary postmodern feminism thus emerges out of the conflicts within feminist theorising and the influence of postmodernist thought. The result is something that presents itself as amorphous, critical, fluid and deconstructive. Some feminists use the term 'deconstructive feminism' as they see the task of contemporary feminism to investigate, take apart and interrogate the elemental make-up of theories such as Marxism and liberalism (as examples of dominant socio-political theories) and to expose their 'latent discursive commitments' (Gatens, 1992: 121). All theories are to be 'deeply interrogated' by deconstructive feminisms which distinguish these contemporary feminisms from their predecessors. Previous feminist theories, such as liberal or Marxist feminism, can be seen as having merely extended 'malestream' theories. Traditional radical feminism cannot be included under the auspices of deconstructive feminism because of radical feminism's apparent belief in a woman's essence or biology as somehow enabling her to produce some sort of pure or non-patriarchal theory (ibid.: 122). Thus contemporary feminisms, whether described as postmodern or deconstructive, are defined by their opposition to both 'malestream' socio-political theories, at least those that are essentialist and totalising, and also feminist theories which share those characteristics. Included in this are the 1970s feminist theories that have been discussed earlier.

Postmodern feminism is thus aligned with the deconstructive strategies of postmodernism in general but has a specific interest in gender and the feminine/female. The point is not to look for the truth about women or gender, as truth cannot be appealed to as the grounds for justice or anything else (like liberation) since it is fully implicated in power relations. Also the point is not to free women from oppression or from oppressive identities as all identities can be oppressive. Freedom, such as it is, consists in 'the happy limbo of non-identity' and in the resistance to categorisation; that is, the resistance, as far as is possible, to the totalising aspects of power and the will to truth (Grant, 1993: 131). The truth about woman, what she is, how she knows – the key questions for traditional feminisms – 'become oppressive notions in themselves for postmodern feminists' (ibid.). The crucial project is to investigate the mechanisms of power that have forged female identities in order to resist identity itself.

Having introduced some of the key themes and ideas of these four categories of feminist thought, I shall move on, in the next chapter, to identify the key issues within feminist modernism and feminist postmodernism that will enable me to evaluate and challenge the idea that there is a gulf between 1970s modernist feminisms and 1990s postmodern feminisms.

## Notes

1 As *The Oxford English Dictionary* explains, the act of being 'exemplary' does not only mean being outstanding or excellent but can also imply that being such a 'model' or paradigm can act as a warning to others.
2 The suffrage movement of the late nineteenth and early twentieth centuries is classically associated with women demanding the right to vote.
3 For the purposes here I shall use the terms postmodernism and post-structuralism interchangeably. Judith Grant also uses these terms interchangeably as 'ways to refer to a loosely affiliated though internally diverse body of thought that has common epistemological and ontological roots in the philosophy of Nietzsche . . . particularly interesting for feminism are the radically social constructivist claims of postmodern theories and the discussions of power, especially as found in the works of Michel Foucault' (Grant, 1993: 128).
4 At the time of writing, Cherie Blair is the wife of the British prime minister (Tony Blair); Ffion is the wife of the leader of the Conservative Party, William Hague.

# 2   The gulf

## Theoretical differences

> Over the last two decades the diversification of feminist theories has
> rendered the rather convenient tripartite division into Marxist
> [socialist] feminism, liberal feminism and radical feminism virtually
> useless.
>
> (Gatens, 1992: 120)

In the last chapter I introduced the four forms of feminism that are the
key players in the alleged gulf between modernist/traditional and post-
modernist/contemporary feminisms. In this chapter I shall go into
more theoretical detail about the nature of some of the differences
between these feminisms, organising the discussion around three key
areas of difference, namely the subject, epistemology and politics.
Many contemporary feminists have claimed that there are sufficient
and significant commonalities between liberal, radical and socialist
feminisms to class them together as modernist and, perhaps more significantly, that there is a large and important gulf between modernist
and postmodernist feminisms. Michelle Barrett and Anne Phillips
have referred to this as a 'gulf' and a 'paradigm shift' (1992: 2);
Linda Alcoff has called it a 'theoretical shift' (1997: 5); Ann Brooks
also writes of a 'paradigm shift' (1997: 8); Annamarie Jagose refers
to 'an anxious moment within feminism' (1997: 126); while Patricia
Ticineto Clough highlights the profoundly troubled nature of feminist
thought brought about by and reinforcing the differences among
feminist theorists (1994: 4).

These scholars generally write about a gulf in terms of the theoretical
differences. At first these presumed theoretical differences between the
feminisms may appear to be unimportant. They may seem to have
nothing to do with our everyday lives. But are theoretical disagree-
ments only academic differences of opinion? Or are they also about

what people do, or might do, or can do, or are enabled or empowered to do? Posing questions like these highlights why it is important to assess this so-called gulf between feminisms. Perhaps we can think about it in the form of a question that many people are seeking an answer to: 'In the face of what is, what should we do?' (Price, 1997: 34).

Feminists have been particularly adept at asking this question. For example, in the face of women being paid less than men for the same work, what shall we do? In the face of women dying because of their sex, what shall we do? There is clearly a difference in the scale and type of problems feminists are faced with. Nevertheless, for many feminists, all 'feminist theorizing is a *writing* to save lives' (Clough, 1994: 6). So asking how the different feminisms help us know *what to do or how to act*, is vitally important because feminist theory is so integrally linked to feminist practice. To say that there is an insurmountable gulf between modernist and postmodernist feminisms implies that different feminist theories or knowledges lead to different feminist practices. And importantly, it is also to imply that these practical differences cannot (possibly even should not) be bridged. In this chapter I want to go into more detail about the theoretical differences between modernist and postmodernist feminisms in order to assess the validity and implications of claims about a gulf between them.

The way I want to start doing this is by introducing some of the fears that modernist feminists have about postmodernist feminists and the initial responses to those fears by postmodernist feminists. In my introduction to postmodern feminism in the last chapter, I mentioned that there has been a certain level of fear bordering on hostility following the use of postmodernism by some feminists (Weeks, 1998: 156). Feminist scholar Jane Flax gives a good example of this and, although it is rather a long quote, I think it is useful to include it here.

> In the Spring of 1990 I was invited to discuss an earlier version of this paper with a group of women who teach in a well-known and successful women's studies program. I had just spent two days as the only woman at another conference at the same university, and I was looking forward to a more friendly and productive exchange. Instead I was quite surprised by the atmosphere of tension and hostility that erupted as soon as I entered the room. The last time I recall experiencing such hostility from a group of expected allies was in 1967 when conflicts about Black Power and the role of whites erupted in the Civil Rights movement. The intensity of feelings and the sense that one's integrity, history,

identity, and place were at stake reminded me of those earlier and equally painful encounters.

(Flax 1993: 131)

Flax goes on to say the sorts of questions and statements that were put to her included: 'You cannot be a feminist and a postmodernist'; 'Post-modernists are apolitical or even antipolitical'; 'They are relativists'; 'Acceptance [of postmodernism] entails abandoning feminism or annihilating its autonomy and force, subordinating it to a deconstructive and inhospitable male-dominated philosophy' (ibid.: 131–132). This encounter and the kinds of questions asked of Flax clearly indicate some level of fear and emotional investment in the debate between modernist and postmodernist feminists. This does seem to imply that something important is at stake, which is why I think it is useful to start by highlighting what some of the main fears are.

## The fears

### Modernists on postmodernists

- Postmodernists have abandoned all belief in the subject, which means that claims for rights on behalf of subjects cannot be made.
- Postmodernists deny there is a 'real truth'. If this is the case, how can anyone ever prove anything is right or wrong?
- Postmodernism cannot provide an agenda for political action and it is apolitical or even anti-political.

### Postmodernist responses to those fears

- Modernists are under the illusion that there are real, a priori subjects on which to make claims to rights.
- Modernists are under the illusion that there is a 'real truth' out there waiting to be discovered.
- Modernists are under the illusion that it is possible to have sure grounds for political action.

I shall take each of these fears and responses and outline modernist feminist views and postmodernist feminist views on each. The way I shall do this is by isolating a central issue within each fear, which can initially be encapsulated in a single word for each; the *subject*, *epistemology* and *politics*. I will deal with each of these issues separately but I need to stress that they are all closely intertwined and impact on each other constantly. We can perhaps think of them as a maypole. A maypole traditionally has a number of ribbons tied to the top of it and several dancers each take hold of a ribbon and go round and round in circles, sometimes passing each other and changing places as they dance, but all the time keeping hold of the ribbons. The effect is that the ribbons become completely entangled. Perhaps this image might be returned to when reading the rest of this chapter bearing in mind that the idea is not so much to try to understand each issue in isolation but to understand how they work together to distinguish modernist feminisms from postmodernist feminisms.

## Modernist feminisms and the subject of woman

*The fear: Postmodernists have abandoned all belief in the subject, which means that claims for rights on behalf of subjects cannot be made.*

The abandonment of subject-based politics is a scary prospect for modernist feminists. Modernist feminist theories generally tell the story that the postmodern deconstruction of the subject of woman threatens women's ability to claim rights on behalf of themselves and other women. This is an appalling prospect for modernists of any persuasion because they believe that the installation of the dignity, worth and authority of the human individual opened up the way for a whole swathe of emancipatory demands leading to all sorts of wonderful benefits. Examples for twentieth-century modernist feminism in the United Kingdom would include the Equal Pay Act (1970) and the Sex Discrimination Act (1975). If the ability to win such rights, or even to ask for them, were to be put in jeopardy by abandoning the subject, it is not surprising that modernist feminists are worried.

To ameliorate this worry, modernist feminists insist that, 'there is such a thing as woman' (Bell and Klein, 1996: xix). They argue that the 'rejection of the subject' (of woman) by postmodern feminists has profoundly bad implications for feminist politics. Some feminists suggest that the deconstruction and loss of the subject 'continues to leave women in a state of fragmentation and dissemination which reproduces and perpetuates the patriarchal violence that separates women' (Whitford, 1991: 123). Additionally some argue that, 'in order to announce the death of the subject one must first have gained the right to speak as one' (Braidotti, 1987: 237). Others argue that to the extent that feminist politics is bound up with a specific constituency or 'subject', namely, women, the postmodernist prohibition against subject-centred enquiry and theory undermines the legitimacy of a broad-based organized movement dedicated to articulating and implementing the goals of such a constituency.

(Di Stefano, 1990: 76)

I shall explain what these concerns mean by providing some background information to modernist feminist thinking about the subject in a moment. To complete my introduction to the 'first fear', I want to highlight and briefly define the central terms at issue here.

---

*The subject – rights – identity (politics) – truth – feminist politics – agency – emancipation – liberation*

---

Again the maypole image should be helpful in trying to understand how all these terms relate to and impact on one another. For modernist feminists, the central *subject* of concern is woman, whose dignity and worth have had to be rescued from centuries of misogynist and patriarchal descriptions. This claiming of the *identity* of woman has been seen as necessary in order to demand *rights* on behalf of her – in current conventional language this has become known as *identity politics*. Other traditionally marginalised groups typically focus on identity politics to gain the rights that groups conventionally not marginalised enjoy. Examples would include black civil rights movements or claims by homosexual couples for the rights and privileges granted to heterosexual couples on marriage.

An important foundation upon which demands for any such rights are made is *truth*. The claim to know the truth of something is profoundly important. Modernist feminists have typically argued that the truth is that women have been unjustly treated and their current state of inequality is a result. They have also argued that women are human subjects worthy of respect and dignity as much as men are, and that claims for 'rights for women' are therefore justified. This all leads to *feminist politics*, which for modernist feminists involves some form of *emancipation* or *liberation* from oppression or simply unfair treatment, resulting in women having control and *agency* in their lives. In a very simple but important sense, modernist feminists want to make women's lives better.

## Making women's lives better

To start clarifying all the above, for modernist feminists, one of the main goals and practices of feminism has been to analyse and understand women's position and condition in society with a view to making women's lives better. In the 1970s and into the 1980s there seemed to be a sense of agreement about this purpose of feminism. 'At one time there could have been a broad consensus that it [feminism] is a body of political ideas reflecting on, and contributing to, the movement for women's liberation from oppression along gender lines' (Coole, 1994: 128). As mentioned above, signs of successful liberation would include equal pay and equal rights plus a whole host of other benefits from protection from male violence to reproductive rights to higher self-esteem and self-confidence. One of the complaints that modernist feminist writers make about postmodernist feminism is that the latter has deviated from the previous consensus about the goals of feminism that, 'all feminists address the same problem – what constitutes the oppression of women and how can that oppression be ended?' (Jaggar, 1983: 124). A key issue over which the consensus has shattered is around the question of the subject, which for modernist feminists has traditionally centred on the category of woman.

Modernist or 1970s feminisms do not simply start with the idea that women just exist and proceed from that point. They can only speak, think and write about women in the way they do because they start out with a fundamental meta-theoretical understanding of the nature of the *subject* or the *self*. In the section on postmodern feminism in the last chapter I introduced Descartes' famous phrase, 'I think therefore I am', as a helpful way to begin understanding modernist ideas about the human subject. This insight of Descartes influenced and structured a whole philosophical way of thinking known as 'Cartesian' which involves a belief in a clear and fundamental separation between 'subjects and objects' (Hekman, 1992: 63). One thing that this implies is that there is a belief in a reality or a real world of objects 'out there' which are not constructed, in significant ways, by our (subject's) understandings or beliefs about them. To put it another way, objects come first and our understanding of and interactions with them come after.

This may seem intuitively correct. Let me give an example. The human body exists and we have consistently tried to understand more about how it works. Of course we can damage or enhance it and generally change it in all sorts of ways, but we generally think that something called 'the body' exists first and our thinking about and understanding of it come later. The example of the body is a rather good one for our purposes in many ways. One is because it is on the female body that many reproductive technologies are practised and therefore I can come back to this example in subsequent chapters. A second and linked example is that attempts to understand how the body works have been very important in the modern era. One of the significant developments since the Enlightenment era has been the growth of modern science, with all the knowledge and technology that go along with it. A driving feature of much modern science has been to 'find out how things work', if possible by finding ultimate explanations in the smallest or one final cause. The biological and medical science of the human body is a paradigmatic example of this, exemplified by the continuing search for 'a gene for everything'.

The media are frequently fired up by the latest 'scientific break-through' story about discovering the 'gene for cancer', or the 'gene for alcoholism' or even the 'gene for sexuality'. In the nineteenth century before genes were 'discovered', chromosomes were similarly used. One theory about the causes of criminal behaviour led to the explanation that when men had an extra X chromosome, this pre-disposed them to behave in criminal ways. One assumption guiding this kind of explanation known as *reductionism* (reducing an explana-tion to the smallest or a single cause) is that there is something 'already there' which has an effect already in place. Thus, for example, a man born with an extra X chromosome will very likely indulge in criminal behaviour. Someone born with the 'gene for homosexuality' will be a homosexual. Of course, each of these individuals might be prevented from carrying out the activities or behaviours associated with being a criminal or homosexual for one reason or another (repression or social expectations, for example), but this does not change what they essentially or naturally are. In this sense, a reductionistic scientific explanation regards the body as an object already in existence and although we can manipulate it and repress its natural tendencies, there is something real and essential to it – a truth – which exists before our thoughts or social practices have any effect on it.

Another example might be the principles of justice. We may argue about them and disagree about who and what should be included, but for modernists, there are real and true principles of justice to be discovered 'out there'. We simply have to get them right. This idea of 'getting it right' is both important and integral to modernist and Cartesian thought. It is important because it is connected to ideas about the truth. And the truth is important because modernists believe that the truth can set us free (from injustice, domination, lies, oppression and so on). That the truth can set us free is a profound idea. In the pre-modern European world, the truth was primarily bestowed by authorities such as the Church or the monarchy or the land or slave-owner. This led to 'truths' such as, it was 'true' that black slave women were only fit for breeding and working; it was 'true' that women practising medicine were witches and therefore deserved to burned at the stake. Generally speaking, in pre-modern times,

> the many found their place and grounded their knowledge in relation to the one who gave or sustained their lives ... the modern self broke away from the defining bodies of the Church and of hereditary social, political and economic power [in theory at least] and as such the individualism of bourgeois subjectivity was genuinely liberatory.
>
> (Scheman, 1993: 186–187)

This sense of liberation was instigated by ideas inspired by philosophers like Descartes, who began to create a whole new way of thinking about the human subject. This helped to displace the authority of the Church and the king and replace it within the individual. This did not mean that religion and monarchies were overthrown – obviously not. It is more to do with ideas about where we go to *find* and *prove* what the truth is. Ultimately, for modernists, it was the capacity of the human subject to *reason* that provided the grounding for truth and certainty; indeed, a central driving force of the modern age has been 'a search for certainty combined with an effort to use reason to establish absolute and universal truth' (Hekman, 1992: 63). From the time of Descartes the search for certainty has been firmly grounded in the rationality and reasoning of the knowing subject or self. This 'knowing self' (which, like 'objects', is understood to exist prior to our understanding or knowledge of it, or any external influences) has been seen, by modernists, as the centre of the human being and the ultimate producer of all truth.

### Her-story

> An early and still common [modernist feminist] response is to claim entry for women into the worlds that men reserved for themselves by hurling a loud 'Me too!' at the wall of arrogance and exclusion.
>
> (Ferguson, 1993: 2)

It may not come as a surprise that feminists discovered that the 'knowing self' has traditionally been male, which led many modernist feminists to be determined to (re)instate women as a subject in history. Quite simply, women have been 'left out' of history; it is men who have been the subjects in history (his-story as opposed to her-story). Liberal feminist calls for equal rights and socialist feminist demands for the recognition of women's (productive and reproductive) work resonate with this view. The radical feminist reclaiming of woman herself is somewhat different to the former two, as there is no desire to be like men or enter the worlds of men. However, each of these three feminist approaches relies upon the division or dichotomy between subject and object characteristic of modernist thought (Hekman, 1992: 78). What this means is that there is, first, a belief in the a priori existence of the subject (woman) and, second, that it is politically important for feminism to bring women into the position of subject-hood. These are some of the primary characteristics of modernist feminisms. If men had reserved the privilege of being the 'rational and knowing self', it seemed logical that women would try to break through the 'arrogant wall of exclusion'.

The recognition of and insistence on women as subjects have allowed for and been the basis of the development of women's identity politics, which has been central in the claiming of rights in the modern era. It is important to remember the ways in which the 'politics of the modern era are anchored upon the notion of a subject' (Elam, 1994: 70). The freedom and destiny of the subject have been a central organising principle underlying contemporary political organisations in the west. This conception of the subject has played an important role in the theory and practice of modernist feminist identity politics. Two examples of how this has manifested itself include the liberal feminist assertion that women and men are essentially and importantly the same (the mind has no sex) and therefore equally entitled to the privileges of subject-hood; and the radical feminist redefinition (or re-discovery) of what women are and the placing of them, as subjects, at the centre. All in all,

> [modernist] feminism understands the subject in terms of identity: the political subject is that which remains identical to itself in the face of contradictions. To be a political subject, then, is to have a political identity, a self, a consciousness to call one's own. What more could a girl want?
>
> (Elam, 1994: 71)

### Agents in action

To be a political subject is indeed, what a 'girl would want' for modernist feminists, as the ownership of 'subject-hood' for women promises
*agency* for women. To have agency is perceived as vital in order to
know what to do, how to act and be able to act. As Elam points out,
'women's attainment of the position of the subject has been seen as a
cause for celebration . . . [especially as] subjectivity seems to offer
agency' (ibid.: 29). Liberal feminists insist that women be recognised
as fully rational beings who can make decisions by and for themselves.
The claim that women are equal to men is based on the belief that only
biology separates the sexes but this is irrelevant to the existence of
rationality, the latter being an essential ingredient of agency. Thus to
give an example of a specific reproductive technology – prenatal screening – this is practised on women as only women have babies, but liberal
feminists argue that women should have the rights and the abilities (on
the proviso of the eradication of sexism and misogyny) to make
rational, autonomous and authoritative decisions about its practice.

Radical feminists, like liberal feminists, believe in an ontologically
prior self (woman) but insist that this self has been distorted out of
all recognition by patriarchy. They have a different view of what
counts as a useful or authentic practice of women's agency than do
liberal feminists. For example, some radical feminists call for a halt
to prenatal screening practices because the latter have emerged from
patriarchal science, technology and medicine, rather than asking for
assistance in using these services more rationally. They might argue
that such technologies are practised on women's bodies merely to
satisfy patriarchal needs for 'healthy' offspring in order to carry forward the male name as well as buttressing the system of compulsory
heterosexuality. Hence the improvement of women's ability to make
rational decisions in this setting is not the overriding concern for radical feminists. Instead they would call for a restructuring of society to
allow women's 'true' selves and needs to be actualised. In this way
women's agency could eventually be *authentically* exercised. For both
liberal and radical feminists, what women *essentially* are is less of a
problem than is the thwarting of (what are believed to be) women's
true needs and desires.

### The amazing disappearing woman

The stability of and belief in the subject of woman has been understood
by modernists as a firm and constructive base from which to start

feminist politics. It makes a great deal of sense, from a modernist perspective, to demand 'rights for women', just as men have. Many modernist feminists are extremely suspicious and sceptical about the loss of the subject instigated by postmodern practices of deconstruction. Some see this deconstruction as a 'kind of theoretical subterfuge to undermine the newly acquired power of marginalised groups' (Waters, 1996: 285). In other words, just as traditionally marginalised groups such as women have begun to gain a voice, the basis on which those voices claim authority is undermined. The loss of the 'female historical agent' may make women vulnerable to all manner of backlashes and leave women 'quite familiarly powerless, filled with self-doubt, unable to assert the ethical necessity and certainty of *anything*' (Chancer, 1998: 26). 'And ain't I a fluctuating identity?' doesn't have quite the same ring to it as Sojourner Truth's poignant plea, 'And ain't I a woman? (Riley, 1988: 1)

## Postmodernist feminisms and the subject of 'woman'

*The response: Modernists suffer from the illusion that there are real, a priori subjects on which to make claims to rights.*

The insistence on subject-based politics is a scary prospect for postmodernist feminists. Many of the latter would agree with modernist feminists that women have frequently been defined as 'inferior' at best or 'a lack' at worst. But postmodern feminists would also argue that since the rise of the 'Cartesian subject', women have still been consistently excluded from its privileges (Hekman, 1992: 79). They insist that this exclusion cannot be remedied by converting women into Cartesian subjects – simply trying to add women in – what must happen instead is a rejection of this definition of the subject (ibid.). Thus for postmodern feminists, it is not a question of *choosing* between retaining the subject or not, rather it is a question of re-visiting our understanding of what the subject is.

If we recall from the previous section, all three modernist feminist approaches rely upon the division or dichotomy between subject and object, implying a belief in the a priori existence of the subject (woman) and the political importance for feminism to bring women into the position of subject-hood. Indeed, 'becoming a subject' has been seen as a great cause for celebration. But postmodernists caution against the urge to 'put on our party clothes too quickly' (Elam, 1994: 29). Why? In order to work through some of the answers to that question, I shall provide some background information on postmodern thinking about the subject in a moment. To complete my introduction to the 'first response', I want to highlight and briefly define the central terms at issue here. Again, it should be useful to bear in mind the maypole image with its many interwoven ribbons.

---

### The subject – categories – representation – undecidability – security

---

Postmodern feminists question the idea of the **subject** on at least two counts. First, they query the idea that there is an essential subject to be discovered. Second, they cast doubt on the political effectiveness of insisting that there is an essential subject of woman within whom identity politics and rights claims can be located. They do not doubt that real women exist or that the **category** of woman is an important one. Why would so much effort be consistently put into defining what woman is (by a whole range of people) if this category were not important? But postmodern feminists argue that there is a big difference between an essential or natural subject and a category.

Rather than trying to assert the truth of the subject of woman, postmodern feminists attempt to show how the category of woman is **represented**. This simply means that they illustrate how the category of woman and ideas about the category are defined, presented and, more often than not, made to appear natural (for example, woman is/as mother). They question the modernist notion that holding on to or believing in a definite idea about what woman is offers **security**, instead arguing that the very **undecidability** of woman paradoxically holds out a great deal of promise in terms of feminist political action.

### Forget the party clothes!

Why is 'becoming a subject' not a cause for postmodern feminist celebration? Let us return to the images of the apple and the onion I introduced in the last chapter. The apple image – representing modernist thinking about the subject – lends itself to ideas about the existence of an 'inner self', whereas the onion image lends itself to notions of a 'constituted self'. All feminists would probably agree that none of us is free from or untainted by societal expectations and demands, so in this sense we are all 'constituted' to some degree. For most modernists the subject is formed through the interaction and intersection of inner (the core) and outer (society) worlds. As such, subjectivity (who we are, how we think, what we feel, what we know) 'is produced not by external ideas, values, or material causes, but by one's personal, subjective engagement in the practices, discourses and institutions that lend significance (value, meaning) to the events of the world' (De Lauretis, 1984: 159).

In simple terms, for modernists there is a 'doer behind the deed' and for postmodernists there is not. In the words of our quintessential postmodern feminist, 'there is no gender identity behind the expression of gender, that identity is performatively constituted by the very "expressions" that are said to be its results' (Butler, 1990: 25). There are at least three implications for feminism arising from the claim that there is no 'doer behind the deed': one is that we can never know what women *really* are as there is no ultimate or essential core to woman; the second is that negative consequences have resulted from insisting that such a core exists; and third that the postmodern eschewal of essential subject-hood for woman does not inevitably imply a negative political stance. Let me explain each of these implications.

### Who are women?

> We do not yet know what women *are*. There are neither epistemological nor ontological grounds which would settle the issue once and for all.
>
> (Elam, 1994: 27)

Attempts have been made (and continue to be made) to define and represent women and come to a conclusion: 'woman is not man'; 'woman is lack'; 'woman/mother'; 'women are sex objects'; 'women are whores'; 'women are pure' and so on. The definitions and representations are wide-ranging. But 'each new attempt to determine women does not put an end to feminist questioning but only makes us more aware of the infinite possibilities of women' (ibid.: 28).

One way of thinking about this is through the image shown on a breakfast cereal packet in which the Quaker Oats man appears on the Quaker Oats box holding a small box, which shows the Quaker Oats man holding a box with a Quaker Oats man . . . and so on infinitely (ibid.: 27). This image opens up a spiral of infinite regression in representation (ibid.: 27). The main point here being that representation can *never* come to an end. If we were to add more detail or information, all we would get is more Quaker Oats boxes. Thus more information would simply lead to more representations – more images – not, as one might think, to better or clearer understandings or knowledges. This infinitely receding and appearing subject means that there is no original woman that has been unproblematically reproduced or fully represented through history; as such women can never be determined as either subjects or objects (ibid.: 29). This seeming 'nothingness' of woman is the essence of the fear modernists have about the loss of the subject. But has imagining that there is an essential core to the subject been such a force for good?

### Women are . . .

Feminists, especially radical feminists, have been particularly good at detailing the objectification of women within patriarchal structures. The illustration of women as victims of violence from genital mutilation to physical beatings to mutilation through dieting and cosmetic surgery is familiar. But if the results of such objectification have led to so many horrors, could subjectification lead to similar horrors?

The key point to get hold of here is one about 'definite' or calculable subjectivity. The achievement of such a measurable subjectivity has not always been a source of liberation. Women have tended to become subjects only when they conform to specified and calculable representations of themselves as subjects, for example as (good) mothers, wives or daughters (ibid.: 29). Subjects 'out of place' can suffer severe sanctions. Recall the example of the suffragettes I used in Chapter 1. These subjects were 'out of place' because they appeared to be demanding rights that only men (by tradition) should demand. And they were vilified for their audacity. Another example is that of the British woman Myra Hindley, who has been serving a prison sentence for playing a part in the murder of children in the 1960s. Her appeals to be released on probation as she has served the sentence of thirty years imposed upon her, have consistently been denied by successive home secretaries. One can claim that her appeals have been denied because public opinion (fuelled by the media) is set against her release because her crimes were so heinous. She is clearly guilty of the crimes she was imprisoned for. But has her sex played a part in making her punishment worse? Does she appear as a woman so much 'out of place' because she helped to murder children? One of the regular arguments put forward by the mother of one of the murdered children is precisely that Hindley is worse than her male accomplice simply because she was a woman and therefore should have responded in a more caring and maternal way to the cries of the children than a man would be expected to. This is perhaps an extreme and controversial example. But there are many other examples which indicate when women are out of place. These will vary over time and culture; one example would include women drinking alcohol or smoking, which has frequently positioned women as 'out of line'.

Returning to the Quaker Oats box image, it may at first glance (literally) seem unsatisfying and frustrating as it appears to be forever going on – there seems to be no 'pinning it down' or stopping it. But the source of frustration is arguably beneficial. The indefinite incalculability can usher in a sense of evasiveness leading to a transformative political effect. If we cannot say what women are or should be, then it will also be difficult to say women are wrong or bad or sinful – or 'out of place'. The infinite uncertainty of who or what woman is means that no matter how many representations of women are made, 'she' will never be filled up (as no matter how many Quaker Oats boxes there are, there will always be another one). This way of phrasing it might appear similar to a traditional patriarchal representation of woman as a lack or emptiness needing to be 'filled up' (invoking further images of heterosexuality – penetrations and filling up of holes, all of which radical feminists might find very unsettling). But the impossibility of 'completing her' or 'filling her in' may simply leave the 'question of woman' open and need not necessarily imply a bar to political action. Indeed, one might argue that too much certainty is more of a threat to emancipation than a help. Consider the simple but profound example of standards of female beauty – a classic way of defining what a woman should be. Such standards have led to 8 year old girls in the west being put on slimming diets or countless years of misery for women worrying about the 'signs of ageing'. Of course, traditional feminists have well portrayed this miserable picture, but then is the answer to replace one definition or certainty about what woman is and should be with another?

### *Ain't I a fluctuating identity?*

> To deconstruct the subject of feminism [woman] is not to censure its usage, but, on the contrary, to release the term into a future of multiple significations . . . paradoxically, it may be that only through releasing the category of women from a fixed referent that something like 'agency' becomes possible.
>
> (Butler, 1995: 50)

It may be the case that 'Ain't I a fluctuating identity?' doesn't have quite the same stirring ring to it as 'Ain't I a woman?' But postmodern feminists would still insist on asking the following question: Does knowing what woman is secure her or ensure she has agency (the ability to act and to know how to act)? Of course it matters who defines what woman is or is supposed to be. I suspect I might prefer a feminist-friendly definition of myself to a misogynist one. But even then, the picture is not quite so clear. What if the feminist definition were one that defined women in opposition to men and insisted that I become a political lesbian, even though I was happily married to a man? Or what if the feminist definition insisted that the measure of contemporary feminist success was to spend most of my time in the world of men and make sure I was acceptable to men, when I really wanted to spend most of my time with women? Or what if the feminist definition of me was one that encouraged me to spend my twenties and thirties working very hard at my career when I really wanted to stay at home with my children, watch old films on television, drink coffee with my friends and have all my expenses paid by my husband?

For postmodern feminists, being tied to specific definitions and expectations, whatever they are or however benign or helpful they are intended to be, can be a hugely restrictive force: 'A modern politics of the subject is not the liberating spirit it may once have been considered to be, and feminism is beginning to recognize the injustices its own political practices have brought about' (Elam, 1994: 76). It is the modernist feminist insistence on the clarity of the subject of woman as a foundation for identity politics and rights claims that has brought about many injustices, according to postmodern analyses. At one time such sure foundations may have seemed the best or even the only political option. But for postmodern feminists the opening up of the question of woman – what she is and is supposed to be – through the practices of deconstruction represents infinite possibilities.

## Modernist feminisms and epistemology

*Postmodernists deny there is a 'real truth'. If this is the case, how can anyone ever prove anything is right or wrong?*

Epistemology is about knowledge. If we ask questions about epistemology, we are usually asking questions like, 'How do we know?'; 'What does it mean to know something?'; 'How do we get to know what we know?'; and even 'Who gets to be a knower?' These are important questions because what gets to be counted as knowledge is linked to claims about 'the truth'. The truth is very important to modernists, as generally what we think of as true has profound effects on our lives. Discovering that Santa Claus is not 'real' can impact upon a child's world in huge ways. If scientists at NASA still believed that the world was flat, this would have major implications for the space programme (would there be one?). And 'knowing' that black people were 'naturally' inferior to white people legitimated centuries of brutal slave ownership. Modernist feminists believe that postmodernism denies that there is anything we can really call 'true'. What might have happened if arguments justifying the abolition of slavery were not taken seriously because there was simply no way to prove that black people had the same rights as white people on the grounds of a common humanity? Before going on to explain this in more detail, I shall highlight some of the main terms at issue in this 'second fear'.

---

*Truth – foundations – objectivity – reality – power – authority – (innocent) knowledge*

---

Discovering and proving the *truth* is of paramount importance to modernist feminists. Being able to prove that women were essentially just as important as men on the grounds of their common humanity has been of massive significance to modernist feminists. By extension, the issue of having grounds for proof is also important and is more usually referred to as *foundations* for knowledge by modernists. The existence of *objective* truth is one of these foundations. Having sure and objective knowledge about the world (the facts) implies that the truth about *reality* can be found. Discovering objective truth means that those who would use power unfairly or unwisely will be kept in check as it will not be *power* or *authority* which decides what is true. Rather, objective truth will 'speak for itself', or in other words, 'the truth will out'. In this way *innocent knowledge* can be gained, which simply means that the knowledge we have about the world, if collected correctly, will be untainted by prejudice or nastiness. Politically, this means that the search for truth holds the promise of one day over-throwing unjust power arrangements like patriarchy.

### Dreaming of innocence

For modernist feminists often dismayed and disgusted by centuries of false and nasty stories about women, the idea that good and true knowledge about women was possible seemed like a dream come true. As I explained in the earlier section on modernist feminist ideas about the subject, there had been a distinct break from believing in the unquestionability or natural supremacy of premodern authorities such as the Church or the monarchy. This resulted in locating the ultimate and authoritative producer of knowledge within the 'rational knowing self'. One of the primary reasons for doing this was to find certainty about puzzles in the world, to have sure and certain knowledge – the absolute truth. This represented a kind of 'Enlightenment dream', the dream being an ultimate solution to the conflict between truth and power. This was a dream (as opposed to a nightmare) because power and authority grounded in pure and wholesome truth would never generate domination, only freedom – at least this is the ideal (Flax, 1993: 134). Modernist feminists, most obviously those influenced by liberal political theory and Marxism, all express some form of this Enlightenment dream.

One way to make that dream come true and ensure that innocent knowledge was collected was to have clear foundations for knowledge-building. Although often unstated, for modernists these will generally include the following beliefs:

- that reality has an objective structure or nature unaffected by or independent of either human understandings of or perspectives on it;
- that the structure or nature of reality in principle is accessible to human understanding or knowledge;
- that a principal human faculty for attaining knowledge of reality is reason;
- that the faculties of reason are potentially the same for all human beings, regardless of their culture or class, race or sex (Jaggar and Bordo, 1989: 3).

These ideas and assumptions are generally accompanied by a dualistic way of thinking about the world. For example, the world is often divided into two sorts of categories such as:

culture/nature
man/woman
mind/body
rational/irrational
subject/object
reason/emotion
good/bad

That we think about the world in these dualistic ways is important in itself but perhaps even more important is that these dualisms are characterised by both *hierarchy* and *opposition*. What this means is that the first term is hierarchically positioned with regard to the second and they are perceived as opposed to each other. In simple terms, good is better than bad and one is the opposite of the other.

Armed with these assumptions, ideas and foundations, modernists believed they were well prepared to identify the best method for people (or 'knowers') to gain knowledge about the world (reality) 'out there'. The paradigm of knowledge for modernists is the physical sciences, which have a distinctive view of what constitutes knowledge and proper scientific enquiry. One of the most important tenets of this paradigm of knowledge to filter through to the social and human sciences is the value of objectivity. There are several aspects to objectivity. First, objectively produced claims are capable, in principle at least, of being verified by anyone; results can either be verified or falsified. A second aspect is that it excludes any evaluative element; empirical observations are the only acceptable data. Values, emotions and interests should be scrupulously avoided as these will bias the findings. Good research will be carried out by detached observers following strict rules and devoid of bias (Jaggar, 1983: 357).

This philosophy of knowledge is founded on a belief in knowledge as a *progressive* force. The more we know about something, the more we understand the truth of it and can do something about it. The popularity of this conception of knowledge since the seventeenth century is hardly surprising, given the rapid increase in knowledge about the world during and since that time. Knowledge about how things work, where things and places are, and how to make new and better things has been prolific in the last 300 years or so. Man has become the important being. It was man's mind, his intellect, significantly assisted by science and technology, that could solve and control the puzzles of the universe.

### But can *she* know?

Modernist feminists might have regarded these foundational tools as a 'dream come true' – but of course there was an obstacle to overcome. The traditional 'knower' or 'knowing subject' of modernism was 'man'. As such, the truth about the world and especially the truth about women, had been arrived at through a mediator – man – and man had distorted the truth: 'Man, ever placed between her and reason, she is always represented as only created to see through a gross medium, and to take things on trust' (Wollstonecraft, 1975: 142). But all was not lost for modernist feminists. Quite the contrary, as they could rely upon the (supposedly) neutral procedures for gathering knowledge in order to eradicate male bias. For example, reason and rationality would prove to be useful tools to claim true and legitimate knowledge of the world – and of women (Hawkesworth, 1990: 119; Tong, 1989: 17).

The importance of knowledge as a tool to understand more about ourselves and the world has been a hallmark of the modern liberal society. A classic example is John Stuart Mill, who wanted the concept of education to be widened to include more than what was being taught in formal institutions, as did Mary Wollstonecraft before him. The path to self-knowledge was deemed to be a glorious one. Liberal feminists of the eighteenth, nineteenth and twentieth centuries accepted this belief in the value of knowledge as self-evident. Indeed, it is fundamental to liberal feminism's epistemology. If we want to gain knowledge about the world, which we do, we simply use existing methodological tools (reason, logic and rationality) and apply them to women and issues of interest and importance to women. Indeed, it is imperative that this be done as falsity has been masquerading as truth. As alluded to above, the truth given to us by men has, in large part, been disguised misogyny. The eradication of misogynist bias is necessary to achieve objective knowledge of the world. If the androcentric (male) bias is removed, then the way will be clear to acquire the truth about ourselves and the world; reality will be perceived clearly (Hawkesworth, 1990: 130–145).

### Women's (special?) ways of knowing

Liberal feminists make no special epistemological claims on behalf of women on the grounds of their sex, only that the same treatment be given equally to all human individuals and the same expectations be made of them, epistemologically speaking. But what of the other modernist feminists? Do radical feminists have a different view of epistemology than liberal feminists?

> Radical feminist epistemology starts from the belief that women know much of which men are ignorant . . . [It also] explores the strategies women have developed for obtaining reliable knowledge and for correcting the distortions of patriarchal knowledge.
>
> (Jaggar, 1983: 365)

This claim about radical feminist epistemology implies that there are at least two important differences between what we can call 'malestream' modernist epistemology and radical feminist epistemology. The first is that women have some knowledges that men either are unable to know or understand or simply don't find interesting or useful to know. The second is that women not only have different knowledges to men, but they acquire it in different ways to men.

What is it women know that men don't? If we recall from Chapter 1, radical feminists claim that men, and not women, decide what counts as important and relevant knowledge in the world and this has been based on the lives and interests of men. But traditionally, women and men lead rather different lives and what is important to men is not necessarily important or relevant to women. Let me give an example by way of an anecdote told about a diplomat.

> A US diplomat working in Britain was asked what he missed most about home, his answer was, 'a good hamburger'. His wife's answer was, 'my job'.

We can read from this anecdote a story about how countless women tailor their lives to fit in with their husband's jobs and how this can result in rather different sets of concerns and interests for men and women. And by the way, before reading the quote, how many of you automatically assumed the diplomat was going to be male?

But, for radical feminists, women not only know and value different things to men by virtue of different lifestyles, they also have different, even special ways of collecting knowledge or understanding the world. Indeed, one might remark that there is a striking difference between radical feminist epistemology and the epistemology of the modernist tradition with the radical feminist acceptance of certain human faculties which are traditionally considered highly unreliable (Jaggar, 1983: 366). These include intuition and spiritual power – both very much the 'opposite' of rationality in the modernist view. These faculties are believed, by many radical feminists especially in the 1970s, to be particularly well developed in women; whether this is inherent or by virtue of the different lifestyles of women is unclear, but these 'womanly capacities' contrast with patriarchal ways of knowing (ibid.: 96). Woman's intuition is both a cause and effect of a special sensitivity to and empathy for others. Spiritual power is said to be a special source of knowledge that is related to women's sense of connection with the earth and nature. As one radical feminist put it:

> We know ourselves to be made from this earth. We know this earth is made from our bodies. For we see ourselves. And we are nature.

> We are nature seeing nature. We are nature with a concept of
> nature. Nature weeping. Nature speaking of nature to nature.
>
> (Griffin, 1980: 226)

Radical feminists like Griffin insist that women generally have different
experiences in the world, different values and crucially different ways of
understanding and knowing the world than do men. Patriarchal
thought is characterised by rigidity, divisions, oppositions and dualisms such as: mind/matter, self/other, reason/emotion. As discussed
earlier, what is particularly important about these dualisms is the hierarchy involved, one the (male) side being valued more than the (female)
other. Radical feminists conclude that hierarchy is built into the foundations of patriarchy (Jaggar, 1983: 367). 'The either/or dichotomy is
inherently, classically patriarchal' as women, and all things female,
were placed either at the bottom half of the artificial hierarchy, or
not placed at all (Morgan, 1977: 15). Radical feminists emphasised
the connection between all things, whether between public and private,
mind and body, fact and value, thought and feeling, theory and practice. One specific practice of knowledge-building and gathering that
this led to for many radical feminists, especially in the 1970s, was
'consciousness-raising groups'. This simply meant groups of women
got together in informal settings to talk about their lives in a supportive
environment. Of course, women have always got together in groups to
chat – but the specific idea behind consciousness-raising (CR) was that
theory grows out of feelings and experience, and that women speaking
together can generate political change (Humm, 1989: 36). The focus on
women having significant commonalities and validating women's personal experiences as a source of authority was a key to ensuring success.

### How special is special?

Although radical feminists rely on some strikingly different ways of
going about collecting knowledge and insisting on the relevance and
importance of women's traditional activities and lifestyles, they retain
a belief in the possibility of ultimately true knowledge. Additionally,
they insist that woman as a subject – even one distorted and abused
by patriarchy – is the correct foundation on which to draw out that
knowledge and truth.

If radical feminists provided the inspiration with regard to feminist
epistemology, one might say that socialist feminists provided the
method. Socialist feminists have typically been keen to 'get the epistemology right'. This has resulted in the development of 'feminist

standpoint epistemology', which is based on a female/feminine subject who *can* know and in very different and arguably special ways to the male/masculine subject. They claim that the social position of women, in other words their different lifestyles and traditions, gives them a special epistemological standpoint which makes possible a view of the world that is more reliable and less distorted than that available to men (Jaggar, 1983: 370).

Feminist standpoint epistemology rests on an idea that human activity not only structures but sets limits on human understanding: what we do shapes and constrains what we can know (Harding, 1991: 120). The central claim reiterated by standpoint theorists is that the majority of knowledge in the world, specifically that produced by institutions of higher education (but one could include all other forms of knowledge production or dissemination such as the media) has been produced largely by elite white men. This knowledge is bound to be partial as it represents only one section of society and the partial vision available to that section. Women's lives differ from men's and hence their perceptions and understandings will differ. Feminist standpoint theorists methodically justify (one might say rationally and logically justify) how and why feminist standpoint theory works. Let me list seven such justifications or grounds for feminist standpoint theory based on the many differences between the situations, lives and experiences of women and men.

1  Women's different lives have been erroneously devalued and neglected as starting points for scientific research and as the generators of evidence for or against knowledge claims.
2  Women are valuable 'strangers' to the social order.
3  Women have less interest in ignorance.
4  Women's knowledge is necessary for the production of less partial and more objective knowledge about social reality.
5  It is preferable, even better, to start research from the lives of women as women's lives are grounded in everyday life (changing nappies and cooking meals as opposed to making boardroom decisions).
6  Women are constantly traversing the divisions, dualisms and separations imposed by western culture.
7  Women are 'outsiders within'.

(Harding, 1991: 121–133)

In keeping with the revolutionary origins of socialist feminism, standpoint epistemology proposes an alternative way of knowing as well as being a revolutionary practice of knowing (Clough, 1994: 62). One aspect of this 'revolution' is that feminist standpoint theorists want to 'redress the male-dominated organization of knowledge by proposing an alternative form of knowing based on women's unique experience of the separation of the private and public spheres' (ibid.: 64).

The point about women's experience of the separation of private and public spheres is an important one. Indeed, it runs through many of the justifications for feminist standpoint epistemology outlined above. Think, for example, of the claims that, 'women are valuable "strangers" to the social order' (2), 'women have less interest in ignorance' (3) and 'women are constantly traversing the divisions, dualisms and separations imposed by western culture' (6). The last claim most quickly gets us to the point about public and private. One of the ideas underlying this kind of claim is again about women and men traditionally and frequently leading different lifestyles resulting in differing interests, values and needs. Working with the originally Marxist insight that human behaviour and activity structure and constrain what humans become ('we are what we do'), feminist standpoint theorists argued that women's regular immersion in 'the everyday' equips them with experiences – and therefore knowledges – about the world that are unavailable to men. For example, women's work is more often located in what we might call the 'bodily mode', whereas men's is more often located in the 'abstract mode'. In other words, women all over the world are constantly involved in the creation and re-creation of the 'dailiness' of everyday life such as cleaning, feeding, washing and childcare. These kinds of 'private' but essential activities enable men to go out into the public world of work as their wives carry out all the messy, time-consuming domestic servicing necessary in order to get them out of the door. This kind of work extends into the public realm also, as women tend to carry out similar servicing functions in the public world of work such as secretarial work, routine computer work and nursing. In constructing an epistemology on the basis of the standpoint discussed above, socialist feminists have posited feminism as a 'position' in society in which reality can be conceptualised from the vantage point of women's lives (Jaggar, 1983: 384; Hennessy, 1993: 67). As this identifiable social group, women have the potential to develop an epistemological position that is different to the dominant (men's) framework but, crucially, at the same time includes that dominant framework (7). This makes them very valuable strangers to the social order (2) because they know how that order works. However, because they are generally oppressed by the social order, unlike men, do not have a burning desire to keep it going. In this way women arguably have a more objective view and less interest in not striving to reach objectivity. Let me give an example of how this might be understood to work.

As I write this there is much media discussion in the UK about the latest crisis in the National Health Service (NHS). The flu epidemic over Christmas 1999 has led to an extreme shortage of beds available in hospitals. Stories of exhausted nurses and dead bodies being stored in refrigerated lorries in hospital car-parks are rife. One radio discussion raised the question of nurses' incomes (it is currently difficult to recruit nurses largely because of poor pay) suggesting that the male manager's income of approximately £80,000 was rather a lot compared to the average £15,000 for nurses (who are still predominately female). Imagine a radical feminist utopia – one in which traditionally female work was highly valued. Perhaps in this world the nurses would be paid £80,000 a year. One can begin to see that it might be easier for women (the nurses in this example) to see the value and use of this argument but not so easy for the male manager, as this might imply his pay would be reduced to £15,000!

The standpoint position as developed by writers such as Nancy Hartsock (1983a, 1983b), Dorothy Smith (1987) and Sandra Harding (1986, 1987, 1991) has been subjected to much criticism, not least because of its empirical reference point of 'women's lives'. First, there seems to be a significant tension between positing knowledge as a construct and yet basing a reconstruction of knowledge on the foundations of a woman-centred experience. A second problem concerns the ubiquitous (in the 1990s) problem of positing a universal or homogenised version of woman.

> Basing feminist knowledge in any transparent appeal to women's experience tends to homogenise 'woman' as a universal and obvious category. It also tends to lock into the structures of feminist epistemology a binary opposition between male and female which naturalises gender and erases the other social categories across which 'woman' is defined.
>
> (Hennessy, 1993: 68)

The problems identified with standpoint epistemology mentioned above are only the start of the criticisms of both the standpoint position specifically and, more generally, the western feminism from which it stems. To be sure, recent standpoint thinking 'seems to have abandoned the idea that there is a unified female identity . . . [and] has moved toward the idea that there are many female standpoints' (Grant, 1993: 91). But from this move, it has proved difficult to maintain 'some notion of Woman' (ibid.). Thus, once again, the reality, concept or subject of 'woman' becomes a problem within feminist theory.

### Still dreaming of happiness

One of the promises of the Enlightenment was that truth would set us free. But, for modernists, unless knowledge has an absolute ground, it cannot qualify as truth (Hekman, 1992: 11). However, conflicts between truth and power could be overcome by grounding claims to knowledge and authority in *reason* which, in turn, promises freedom. For those feminists influenced by liberalism, legitimate authority is distinguished from domination by obeying the rules of reason. For those feminists inspired by Marxism, objective grounds are to be found in history, which is ultimately rational, purposive, unitary, law-governed and progressive (Flax, 1993: 134). The plausibility, coherence and intelligibility of these claims depend on a number of (again usually unstated) assumptions already discussed. Significantly, they include a belief that truth and prejudice are clearly distinguishable and dichotomous categories, and that there is a neutral language available to report our discoveries about the truth of the world.

Modernist feminists fear that postmodernism will call a halt to those promises and aspirations. Their fear is such, that despite the problems of epistemologies based on the rationality and neutrality of modernism or on women and women's experiences, the alternative putatively offered by postmodernism is not acceptable to modernist feminists: 'Postmodernist discourse is constituted by a series of attempts to close doors or paths back to Enlightenment modes of thinking or promises of happiness' (Flax, 1990: 189). Turning a postmodern back on the progressive ideas and values of the Enlightenment and putting forward the idea that no one can really be a 'knower', or that the truth of the 'known' is an illusion, will (literally) send us back to the dark ages and irresponsible power will once again rule. So for modernist feminists, postmodernism cannot provide a politically usable epistemology (Scheman, 1993: 189). And for modernist feminists, it is important to 'rescue feminist claims from trivialisation by demonstrating their truth and importance' (Hawkesworth, 1990: 130). Additionally, 'should postmodernism's seductive text gain ascendancy, it will not be an accident that power remains in the hands of the white males who currently possess it' (ibid.: 148).

## Postmodern feminisms and epistemology

*The response: Modernists suffer from the illusion that there is a
'real truth' out there waiting to be discovered.*

Postmodernists agree with modernists about the profound importance
of the truth. The former are also keenly interested in the same kinds of
questions such as, 'How do we know?', 'What gets counted as truthful
knowledge?' and 'Who gets to be considered a "knower"?' But unlike
modernists, postmodernists are not interested in reaching and proving
the truth and finding the ultimate 'real' answers to those questions. This
is because they do not believe in the idea of truth in the same way as
modernists. Postmodernists claim that 'one real truth' about anything
is an illusion. However, what is vastly important is that things come to
be understood as true. Postmodernists see their task as working out
how this belief in the truth of things comes about and investigating
what it does. This does not mean that things (like women, knowledge,
power) don't exist, but is that what really matters about anything is the
meaning that it comes to have. A china cup can be a drinking utensil
and so if it gets broken it may not matter very much. But the same
object might be a container for the ashes of a dead loved one and as
such the consequences of dropping it can be very different. If the
'dead one' were a king or god and the punishment for dropping the container were execution, then the consequences would be extremely different. That it is the same object is, in any meaningful way, irrelevant.
Before explaining in more detail, let me introduce the main terms at
issue in this 'second response'.

---

*Power/knowledge – privilege – language – difference – deconstruction –
de-naturalisation*

---

As explained earlier, knowledge and truth are intimately linked and for
modernists the separation of power and truthful knowledge is vitally
important in order to have the best possible chance of liberating
people from prejudice, discrimination and downright evil. In contrast,
postmodernists argue that power and knowledge are not mutually
exclusive and instead think of them as joined and mutually reinforcing,
hence the intertwined expression; *power/knowledge*. In other words,
postmodernists do not accept that 'innocent knowledge' is possible
(as modernists do). All knowledge emanates from a position of
*privilege*; all standpoints rely on ideas and beliefs that are not neutral

but privileged, whether that is man's 'natural' authority, woman's 'special ways of knowing' or the 'neutrality' of rationality. Privilege conceived in this way is not meant to imply superior advantage; rather it means non-neutrality. Because postmodernists do not think of power and knowledge as separate, they do not spend time asking the typical modernist question, 'How can we find true knowledge?' Instead, postmodernists generally ask 'How does power construct the truth?'

One place in which postmodernists look to find illumination on this question is in the area of *language*, as this is a powerful arena where meaning is made and transmitted. Postmodernists investigate language as something that is not a neutral transmitter of meaning but as something that creates a system of *difference*. This system is the one of dualistic hierarchies identified by modernist feminists: culture/nature; man/woman; good/bad and so on. Traditionally we think of language as a tool to help distinguish each of these terms from the other. However, postmodernists argue that power is infused in the language we use and does not so much describe or explain each term neutrally but provides the meaning for the term. One technique or method used to investigate these infusions of power and show how meaning is constructed is *deconstruction*.

Postmodernists using deconstruction agree with modernists that dualisms are built on hierarchical oppositions. But instead of suggesting that the more valued term oppresses the other, deconstruction shows the interdependence of the terms. In other words, the valued term is dependent upon and infused with the less valued term. This implies that without the term 'woman', 'man' means nothing; or that 'heterosexuality' depends upon 'homosexuality' for its meaning and therefore its existence. At some level, this is something we all know, especially feminists. What postmodernists add is an analysis which shows how these hierarchies work by deferring this knowledge we all know. For postmodernists, knowledge is not repressed (as modernists think), nor is it retained, it is constantly deferred – it always seems to be slipping out of reach. Postmodern deconstruction investigates how this postponement of knowledge or 'not knowing' occurs. One of the consequences and aims of deconstruction is to *de-naturalise* things that have become naturalised. This is again linked to the issue of meaning as postmodernists argue that things, facts, ideas, beliefs or concepts don't have any natural or inherent meaning in and of themselves. Instead, their meanings come from infusions of power. At first glance many of these ideas appear very complicated. They are seen as all the more complex and unusual precisely because they are not established or conventional ideas in the way that modernist arguments and ideas are. All will hopefully become clearer as we go along.

### Innocent knowledge? Forget it!

A central target for postmodernists is the (naïve?) dream of the Enlightenment. For postmodernists there is no foolproof method of separating truth and knowledge from power, or of separating prejudice from neutrality. What becomes counted as a reasonable or rational explanation must, at some point, depend upon selective definitions about what counts as reasonable, rational, neutral or truthful. 'There is no standard of rationality that we have not created ourselves' (Rorty, 1982: xiii). The postmodernist suspicion of the notion that truth can be rescued from power is largely inspired by the work of Michel Foucault (1967, 1972, 1975, 1977, 1979). Foucault's work on power and its relationship to knowledge rejects the conventional modernist understanding of power as simply *repressive*. The modernist story is familiar. Power is something people have and power can be and is regularly used to thwart or oppress people's needs, interests, knowledges and desires. There are obvious ways in which this happens. A parent has power over a child and can force him or her to do things against the child's will. This might be done by instilling a sense of fear in the child – by the threat of physical punishment for example – or by invoking feelings of guilt, duty or love. This relationship of power usually changes over time, but the modernist idea is that the *balance* of power alters; the parent loses some power and the child gains some power. Another example on a broader scale might be that of an oppressive political regime whereby the leader deals with opponents, dissidents and 'undesirables' by killing them or having them 'disappear'. General Pinochet's regime in Chile is commonly seen in the west as a prime example of this. Hitler's Nazi regime and Pol Pot's regime in Cambodia are other examples.

In the specific context of epistemology and the production of truth and knowledge, the classic modernist aim is to release truth from power. But for postmodernists, especially those following Foucault, 'it's not a matter of emancipating truth from every system of power . . . for truth is already power' (quoted in Rabinow, 1991: 74–75). Following this, the idea of repression, for postmodernists, is quite inadequate to capture what the productive aspects of power are or how it works. Foucault's way of explaining this is by saying that thinking about power as repressive, identifies power with a law which says no; power is taken above all as carrying the force of a prohibition . . . [I]f power were never anything but repressive, if it never did anything but to say no, do you think one would be brought to obey it?

(Quoted in Rabinow, 1991: 60–61)

Foucault argues that power is not something that just says 'no', but is something that forms knowledge and which needs 'to be considered as a productive network which runs through the whole social body, much more than as a negative instance whose function is to repress' (ibid.: 61).

I am using Foucault's own words here rather a lot as he has been so influential on postmodern thinking about power and the connections with knowledge. Additionally, I am using these extracts from an interview with him as I think the interview format often encourages people – especially those expressing radical or seemingly unusual ideas – to explain those ideas in an accessible way. Let me use one more quote from him.

Truth isn't outside power, or lacking in power . . . truth isn't the reward of free spirits, the child of protracted solitude, nor the privilege of those who have succeeded in liberating themselves . . . Truth . . . is produced only by virtue of multiple forms of constraint.

(Ibid.: 72)

### What's true? What's new?

One problem that postmodernists making these kinds of arguments face is that their arguments do not sound intuitively correct in a contemporary western setting. Paradoxically, they can also sound as if they are saying nothing different to any other critical theorist. For example, modernists may claim that it simply must be true *and* just to find the correct arguments defining the enslavement of black people as morally wrong. Think of the steps such a discussion about this might take. In the southern states of seventeenth-century America, a black abolitionist could try and persuade a wealthy land- and slave-owner that slavery was wrong on the grounds of common humanity. However, the slave-owner could simply reply that blacks did not share the same humanity as whites, indeed they were more like animals. Now, with our contemporary modernist ideas about finding the correct answer (based on any number of things, including scientific knowledge or the principles of justice and human rights), we could convincingly claim that the argument that blacks were more like animals was wrong. Additionally, given the positive benefits of the truth of such an argument (ending slavery), for modernists it seems vitally important to have sure and accurate foundations for making those claims (science, the principles of justice and human rights and so on). Therefore, arguing that truth is an illusion seems intuitively wrong to the contemporary western modernist mind-set. Just like saying 'Ain't I a fluctuating identity?' seems 'empty' alongside the plea, 'Ain't I a woman?'; so might claiming that 'The truth of a common humanity for blacks and whites is produced only by virtue of multiple forms of constraint' compared to 'Blacks have the right to the dignities of humanity'.

Yet a contemporary western, critically thinking modernist would also see how power played an important part in all these arguments. For example, if the person arguing against slavery were black, his or her arguments would automatically hold less authority by virtue of the fact that centuries of prejudice had repressed the belief in the worth of anything that black people had to say, especially in the context of resisting white oppression. And, of course, the consequences of agreeing with the arguments against slavery were not in the interests of the slave-owner, which provided an additional reason for denying their validity. So it is not accurate to say that modernists do not see power playing a major role. But the modernist aim, as explained already, is to distinguish truth from power in order to release those who are oppressed by prejudice from their oppression. We must remember that postmodernists are not trying to distinguish truth from power as truth is not outside power. How does power produce truth? One way is through language.

### What's in a name?

Desdemona:  Am I that name, Iago?
Iago:      What name, fair lady?
Desdemona:  Such as she says my lord did say I was.

(*Othello*, Act IV, scene ii)

Names are vastly important and by 'name', I mean to imply a broad usage of the term. To analyse 'naming' critically is not simply to examine the 'superficial' names we call people, although this is not unimportant. Think of the difference between naming a boy 'Sue' and a girl 'Charlie'. Or the damage caused and prejudice entrenched by calling black people 'niggers' or by calling homosexuals 'queers' in the 1950s. However, postmodernist analysis of naming implies a fundamental analysis of the constitutive nature of language. To start understanding this, we need to know something about the work of Ferdinand de Saussure (1974).

Saussure undermined the dominant view that language expressed universal truths linguistically. Language, far from reflecting an already given social reality, constitutes social reality for us (Weedon, 1987: 22). Different languages and differences within the same language divide up the world and give it meaning in different ways that cannot be reduced to a fixed and universally shared concept of reality. Saussure's theory of the 'sign' is important in understanding postmodernist ideas about language. For Saussure, language is an abstract system consisting of chains of signs. Each sign is made up of a *signifier* (sound or written image) and a *signified* (meaning). The two parts of the sign are related to each other in an arbitrary way and there is no natural or inherent connection between the sound image and the concept it identifies. Thus the meaning of signs is not natural or inherent but relational. Signs get their meaning from differences to other signs. Nothing intrinsic to the signifier 'whore', for example, gives it any meaning. Instead, it is the difference from other signifiers of womanhood such as 'virgin' or 'mother' which provides the meaning (ibid.: 23).

Postmodernists generally agree with Saussure that meaning is produced within language rather than reflected by language. Whereas Saussure argued that the meaning of signs become fixed according to the conventions of the 'speech community', postmodernists claim that meaning is never fixed but constantly deferred. The work of Jacques Derrida is important in this context (1976, 1979, 1981, 1992). Derrida argues that there can be no fixed signifiers or concepts; the meanings are endlessly deferred and referred. This can be understood in a similar way to the 'Quaker Oats Box Man' image discussed in the section on postmodernism and the subject. The meaning of the signifier 'woman' is always on the move (victim, whore, madonna, mother) and therefore open to challenge and redefinition (Weedon, 1987: 25). Unlike modernists, postmodernists do not desire to fix the meaning of signifiers or concepts but to investigate how the meanings become fixed and to illustrate the effects of these fixings.

If we think about some of the examples I have used – nigger, queer, madonna, virgin – it may become easier to understand the postmodern case for 'meaning always being on the move'. In the 1950s and 1960s the words 'nigger' and 'queer' were clearly understood as insulting descriptions of blacks and homosexuals. In the late 1990s both of these words have, in part, been reclaimed by the communities they were once applied to as insults. Phrases such as, 'niggers with attitude' or 'we're here, we're queer, get used to it!', are evidence of the signifers having 'moving meaning'. Of course, from a modernist perspective, fixing the meaning in an emancipatory way is beneficial. But not so for postmodernists: fixing the meanings – whatever the meaning – is problematic. For example, during the coal miners' strike in Britain in 1984/85 the fundamental conflict of interests led to a situation in which the actions of the trade unionists, the police and the politicians were given radically different meanings by various interest groups. The miners, for example, were simultaneously presented as criminal thugs and ordinary decent men fighting for a living wage for their families, whereas the police were seen as both upholders of the law and agents of class interest fighting an immoral battle against their fellow workers. Trying to create a coherent and fixed 'truth' about either of these groups only led to a hardening of positions between striking and working miners, the police and politicians which prevented any shift in power relations (ibid.: 21–22).

### Marriage, co-habitation or impending messy divorce?

Where does feminism come into all this? Feminists have an interesting and often difficult relationship with postmodernism. Modernist feminists have consistently attempted to prove that feminist claims were right, true and just. But if there is no such thing as objective knowledge, or objective foundations for knowledge, how can feminist demands be proved? Additionally, what about the reliance, once again, on the ideas and theories of men – some seemingly anti-women if not down-right misogynist. One of Nietzsche's infamous lines is, 'thou goest to woman? Remember thy whip!'[1] Or Derrida's judgement that '[Woman] seduces from a distance. It is thus necessary to keep one's distance from women' (1979: 49). On the other hand, some feminists are postmodernists themselves and will therefore be working with ideas and concepts in the realms of non-foundationalism, non-subject-based politics and anti-epistemology. Can feminism and post-modernism be married up – especially in the realm of epistemology?

For most modernist feminists the answer is a resounding 'no'! The reasons given for this answer include the by now familiar arguments about needing a sound and firm base on which to make claims to knowledge. And of course for some modernist feminists, this implies a specific brand of epistemology – feminist standpoint. Feminist post-modernists reject the possibility of foundations as well as the possibility of superseding one privileged epistemological position (masculinist)

with another (feminist). This practice both continues to work within the
dualisms and also imagines that the hierarchy upon which the dualism
is structured can be overturned. This perhaps is the modernist hope –
but postmodernist feminists do not think this is possible. The postmodern argument is that, 'only a move that dissolves the dichotomy
can successfully remove that prescribed inferiority' (Hekman, 1992: 42).

This idea about the hierarchy being embedded within the dualism
alongside the constitutive nature of language can be nicely shown by
the following example. Think of some of the arguments about dispos-
ing of toxic waste. One such argument might be that a corporation
should stop dumping toxic waste because it is damaging the creations
of mother-earth. Another might be that the corporation should
stop dumping toxic waste because it is calculated that it is causing
\$8.215 billion of damage to eight nonrenewable resources, which
should be seen as equivalent to lowering the GDP by 0.15 per cent
per annum (Cohn, 1994: 230). In a western context, the first argument
is paradigmatically associated with femininity and the latter with
masculinity. In a second context of gender hierarchies, this necessarily
implies that the 'feminine' argument is less valued than the 'masculine'
one. Once again, the postmodern argument would be to dissolve the
dichotomy itself.

## An Enlightenment nightmare?

Under the rhetoric of 'defending freedom and justice', modernists,
according to postmodernists, are simply justifying another system of
conquest. The latter argue that modernist epistemological foundations
are dangerous as they posit the existence of the 'true' and the 'real' in the
name of the neutral use of reason or the objective laws of history, yet
they conceal a quest to 'master the world conclusively by enclosing it
within an illusory but absolute system' (Flax, 1993: 137). Additionally,
'modernity, the postmodern voice says, is about conquest . . . [It] is
about silencing others in a sort of theoretical imperialism . . . [Reason]
is a weapon to exclude and silence' (Marshall, 1994: 24).

This whole story around truth and foundations for truth is described
by postmodernists as a meta-narrative; 'the absolute justifying mechanisms of foundational thought' (Rorty, 1983: 585). Introducing another
meta-narrative, one based on woman, women, or feminist standpoint
epistemology is not the answer according to feminist postmodernists.
Although this does not have to imply an inability to 'do politics' or
to 'be political', it does clearly imply that modernist feminists and postmodern feminists have different views about what counts as politics.

## Modernist feminisms and politics

***The fear: Postmodernists cannot provide an agenda for political action and thus it is apolitical or even anti-political.***

Most feminist scholars agree that feminism has a political agenda or is political (Grant, 1993: 149; Weedon, 1987: 1; Elam, 1994: 67). However, as will become clear, there are differences of opinion about what 'being political' entails. As explained already, modernist feminists insist on the necessity of retaining the subject of woman as well as insisting on the fact that women have much in common in order to organise collectively and to achieve concrete results, such as the right to vote, equal pay and the achievement of reproductive and sexual rights. Enshrining these rights in the law sets an important and necessary seal. Modernist feminists fear that postmodern approaches do not properly recognise the need for this sort of concrete political struggle and clear agenda to gain material changes (Scheman, 1993: 189). Partly as a result of the impact of postmodernism on feminism over the last few decades, some feminists have recently suggested that it is now desirable to 'revitalise the original agenda of second-wave [modernist] feminism as committed to the practical liberation of women' (Oakley, 1998: 133). I shall explain all this in more detail subsequently. Let me first highlight and briefly explain the central terms at issue in this 'third fear'.

---

*Politics – political agenda – consensus – identity politics – practical action – concrete results*

---

Modernist feminists would claim that in order for *politics* to happen, a *political agenda* or project is required. Such an agenda or project usually consists of a 'wish list' of needs, wants and desires as well as agreement as to how to go about getting what is on the wish list. For modernist feminists, such a list has included the right to vote, to have equal pay and to have equal opportunities in the sphere of paid employment. To ensure that demands like these have the best possible chance of success, it is important that a *consensus* be reached about the problems which have led to such demands having to be made (patriarchy, misogyny or outdated beliefs for example) as well as to the content of the demands themselves.

A form of group identity or *identity politics* is generally perceived as a necessary base from which to start creating or reaching such a consensus. For modernist feminists it has been vital to see women as a group with interests and inequalities or oppressions in common and to demand rights and justices on behalf of that group. In western liberal democracies, seeking changes through the law has been a significant forum through which such demands have been made. But other forms of *practical action* have been carried out by modernist feminists. For example, there are 'reclaim the night' marches, which are marches at night peopled mostly by women meant as a statement about the fear many women have about going out alone at night; organising battered women's shelters; and simply being supportive to other women by taking women's experiences seriously. Through such practical action it is hoped that *concrete results* will be achieved, such as legislative changes enshrining equal rights in the law or the construction of an environment in which all women feel safe to go out alone at night. Women's total liberation from the inequalities and oppressions caused by sex discrimination and erroneous beliefs about gender differences would be the ultimate concrete result for modernist feminist politics.

### So what counts as politics?

Postmodernism obviates the possibility of committed political action and, most particularly, action that is guided by the Enlightenment's goal of emancipation.

(Hekman, 1992: 154)

For modernist feminists there clearly must be firm bases on which to make political demands on behalf of women with clear results, for example legislation. But many modernist feminists have importantly expanded what counts as political. The effects of the claim that 'the personal is political' is largely responsible for this. Of course it is radical and socialist feminists who have been primarily responsible for insisting that 'the personal is political'. But it might also be argued that the logic of many liberal feminist arguments leads to a similar position about the political nature of the private realm. In the light of this, some feminists have argued that liberal feminism has a radical future (Eisenstein, 1986) 'not least in challenging the separation and opposition between private and public spheres' (Pateman, 1989: 119). Defining rape in marriage as a violent act, or domestic violence as a crime, or showing that the socialisation of girls and boys into 'appropriate' gender roles is a political manoeuvre have been important victories for modernist feminists. Additionally, so has campaigning for reproductive rights or for equal pay, which all seems so much more 'real' and concrete for modernist feminists. Conversely, the endless questioning of concepts, ideas and theories typical of postmodernism, 'contributes nothing to any political enterprise committed to challenging domination, and at worst, actively undermines it' (Thompson, 1996: 326). The postmodern refusal to name domination through its abandonment of master-narratives together with its anti-subjectivity and distrust of the progressive values of the Enlightenment makes feminist postmodernism 'incapable of political engagement' (ibid.: 337). What feminists really need is to 'get in on the action'.

### 'Getting in on the action'

To explain about 'getting in on the action', let us recall the last stanza of the poem, *The Socialist and the Suffragist*, from Chapter 1, in particular the last line.

> The world awoke and tartly spoke:
> 'Your work is all the same;
> Work together or work apart,
> Work, each of you, with all your heart
> *Just get into the game.*'

The 'game' in the story of the poem involves a debate about who has the greater claim to rights – working classes or women – because of economic and sexual injustice. The conclusion – 'just get into the game' – indicates that what really matters is 'getting in on the action', rather than arguing about who has the greater claim.

Modernist feminists have clearly wanted to 'get into the game', the 'game' being a political one in which feminist voices and demands can be heard and responded to. Each of the three modernist feminisms I am looking at approaches 'the game' in somewhat different ways. For example, as we have seen, liberal feminists have campaigned and lobbied for a variety of things, including the inclusion of women into education, the professions and party politics. They have historically based their claims on the rights of women (as equal, reasoning beings) and the injustice of unfair discrimination. Socialist feminists have clearly wanted to get into the public political game as a way to expose and ameliorate the inequities of the class structure. Using Marxist analyses of 'class', women were defined by these feminists as a class with interests in common and, as such, sharing the ground necessary in order to fight battle against oppression. On the other hand, radical feminists have not wanted to get into quite the same game. For example, one can easily imagine liberal feminists becoming members of parliament and working within that system. One can similarly imagine socialist feminists, especially post-1989, doing the same, even if the latter were trying to change that system in more ways than a liberal feminist might. Radical feminists would not want to enter the same traditional public political environment. However, they do want to enter – and win – the same kind of meta-theoretical game. In other words, they want to prove that their claims about oppression and discrimination against women are true and that there should be concrete changes within society and to women's lives in order to redress these inequities. One thing that is noticeable about modernist feminist debates is that all these feminists speak about a group of people called women.

### Back to women

> One cannot meaningfully theorize about – or politically organize – a group of people one cannot define: how, we are asked, can there be a movement for women's liberation if we cannot define what is meant by 'woman', if we cannot tell who is and who is not one?
> (Scheman, 1993: 191)

'Doing politics' for modernist feminists is therefore centrally about constructing theories on behalf of *women* in order to make women's lives better. It follows therefore that the identity of woman and women is a necessary foundation. Losing this foundation would be a luxury feminists cannot politically afford. Modernist feminists argue that without an ontologically and epistemologically grounded feminist subject, there can be no politically effective action. Some claim that the recent emphasis on the differences between women disempowers women as it prevents a discussion of similarities, or the common oppression of woman, which is an essential part of modernist feminisms (Hirschmann, 1992: 330). Of course there are differences between women, but many would argue that it is politically necessary to put these differences aside in the name of coalition building. For many modernist feminists, the 'de' in deconstruction takes away the possibility of making constructive moves in the political realm (Scholes, 1989: 94). In short, these feminists argue that it is epistemologically and politically necessary to say 'we' in order to achieve concrete results in the realm of practice.

## Postmodern feminisms and politics

*The response: Modernists confuse the ability to provide an agenda for political action with securing sure grounds for political action.*

If modernist feminists are frightened of a retreat from the emancipatory utopia promised by the Enlightenment (Benhabib, 1992: 230), and the loss of a satisfactory politics (Alcoff, 1997: 8) as a consequence, postmodern feminists are extremely sceptical of the claims made by the former as to what counts as 'proper politics'. Modernists may be positioned as defenders of freedom, truth and justice and being political fighters on behalf of the oppressed, but postmodernists claim that modernist certainties are simply another form of oppression. These claims lead postmodernists into some very tricky territory in several ways. One is that people generally seem more comfortable with certainty than with doubt or confusion and so resist the postmodern leaning towards endless questioning and displacement, which can make them feel uncomfortable. Indeed, Descartes wrote about the despair of doubt and the peace of certainty (Cahoone, 1996: 29). A second tricky issue is to do with the idea that modernism once 'defied the cultural order of the bourgeoisie . . . today, however, it is the official culture (Foster, 1985: ix), especially in western social/liberal democracies and in academic theorising generally.

Overall, people still believe that the search for truth and sure knowledge is a good and noble cause and that defying such an 'official' stance, or any official culture for that matter, can be very uncomfortable and appear too rebellious. But defy it they do, as we have seen in the area of the subject and epistemology and now in this third arena of politics. All this raises the important question: Are postmodern strategies a responsible way to do feminist politics? Of course postmodernists believe the answer to this question is yes, and they additionally think that it is really modernist strategies that amount to irresponsible feminist politics. Before going on to explain this, let me identify the key terms at issue in this 'third response'.

---

*Power/resistance – authority – deconstruction – the political – effects – responsibility*

---

A typical postmodern claim is that power is not something that is simply or only repressive. In keeping with a desire to dismantle dualistic thinking, postmodernists refuse to perceive power as fundamentally opposed to resistance, hence the intertwined phrase; ***power/resistance***. Indeed, the idea that there is a monolithic power 'out there', whether that is patriarchy, racism or capitalism, can lead to a sense of fatalism and despair, which is hardly the best way to achieve emancipatory ends, postmoderns might argue. This links into the notion of productive power introduced earlier, which implies that the persistent battle over the meanings of things will inevitably foster new forms of resistance and new meanings emerge from this. The battles over the words 'queer' and 'nigger' serve as good examples of this. The consistent postmodern emphasis on disputing meanings and displacing traditional ideas and values, inevitably leads to a questioning and dishevelling of modernist definitions and certainties about what counts as politics. This imposition of the ***authority*** of correct meaning is something that postmodernists are keen to expose.

Postmodernists also resist the idea that their views of the subject and epistemology lead to an inability to be political or do politics. If we think of a specific postmodern method, ***deconstruction***, we can understand it as something that questions the terms in which we understand ***the political***, rather than an abandonment of the political. Surely, postmodernists argue, questioning what counts as politics is a political act? Rethinking what the political is can allow a whole range of differences of opinions to appear. Additionally, rather than concentrating on the 'why' of things, postmodernists prefer to focus on ***effects***. So instead of asking, 'Why are women oppressed?', postmodernists are more likely to ask questions about the effects of particular practices. For example, 'What are the effects of beliefs about the "proper" roles for women such as those espoused by the Catholic Church?' Or in other (postmodern) words, 'How do women get said [or described] as "good wives" by the Catholic Church?' Questioning foundations, beliefs about who and what 'the subject is' and opening the notion of politics surely counts as taking feminist ***responsibility*** seriously?

### So how does postmodern feminism 'do politics'?

> If we do our work well, 'reality' will appear even more unstable, complex and disorderly than it does now.
>
> (Flax quoted in Hekman, 1992: 158)

How is what Flax suggests a responsible act in the context of feminist politics? As should be clear by now, given postmodern feminist views on the subject and epistemology, these feminists disagree with modernists that we can ultimately ground our knowledge about who or what woman is. The politics that follows from such modernist certainties is an unnecessarily limited one. For example, postmodernists argue that modernists understand politics to be a 'representational discourse that presumes a fixed or ready-made subject, usually conceived through the category of woman. As a result, analysis of the political construction and regulation of this category is summarily foreclosed' (Butler and Scott, 1992: xiv). A central suggestion here is that modernist feminists have made some very clear decisions about where to 'stop the meaning'; one is that the subject of woman is the correct basis for feminist politics. The certainty with which they believe this implies, for Butler and Scott, a limiting of political action. In other words, modernist feminists have decided what women are (rational agents, dupes of patriarchy or alienated humans, for example) and base their explanations and political agendas on this. For modernists, then, there are some very clear 'stopping places' with regard to how far one thinks the 'becoming a woman' extends. Following this, all three modernist groupings rely on some form of identity politics which indicates a pre-commitment to dissolve or ignore differences between women at some point in order to claim rights and form coalitions. And, as discussed earlier, each modernist group believes in some essential, ultimate core to the subject of woman. Leading from this each group of feminists can insist that they know what women are and what women want.

On the other hand, postmodern feminists try not to have any 'stopping places'. This implies several things. One is that there is no desire to uncover what woman is or to decide what she is. Another is that there is an endless desire to discuss and deconstruct the endless representations of woman and women; *not* to expose a 'real' representation at some point down the line but simply to show how woman is the effect of discourse, language and power – illustrating how women 'get said'. For feminist postmodernists, stopping the meaning of something is a political act and thus it is imperative that persistent attempts are made to 'stop the meaning being stopped'. This will inevitably lead to an increased sense of instability, complexity and disorder – but as a result of feminist postmodern insistences on the political importance of this work. They claim that the uncertainty that results from the abandonment in the belief in the subject does not necessarily lead to a situation of political stasis. 'The indeterminacy of women is no cause for lament; it is what *makes* feminism' (Riley, 1988: 114). Women have been 'called' so many things. And by this I mean that many decisions have been made with regard to what women can do or are 'supposed to be' – women have been given so many 'names'. Or as Luce Irigaray articulates it, 'Try to go back through the names they've given you . . .When you stir, you disturb their order. You upset everything. You break the circle of their habits . . . their knowledge, their desire' (Irigaray, 1985: 205, 207). Unsettling the (patriarchal?) 'order' – exposing the indeterminacy of woman, on this view, is clearly a destabilising political act.

## But we can still speak of 'women'

As Simone de Beauvoir classically stated it, 'One is not born a woman, one becomes one.' This assertion, for Flax, is one of the most radical ever made within feminist theorising (Flax, 1993: 23). In a profound way, all feminists probably agree with de Beauvoir. But this 'indeterminacy' or 'endless becoming' does not mean we cannot speak about women. Instead it means that essentialist and reified versions of women are resisted, for example that all women should be good mothers or exist only to satisfy male desires. Postmodern feminists argue that discussing representations of women has great political potential as it leaves open the question of what woman is rather than tying it down to some definite rules which inevitably will be broken (how many perfect mothers are there out there?). Trying to close down these questions, whether by feminists or misogynists, has been problematic for women. Uncertainty (about what woman is) is neither an obstacle to action nor a theoretical bar to political praxis. Being uncertain about what a 'good mother' is leaves space for women to decide for themselves what might count as good mothering. Too much certainty and false beliefs offering 'easy answers' are perceived as dangerous by postmodern feminists. This can seem hopelessly apolitical, even immoral to modernist feminists. The latter argue that it is politically necessary to discuss real women's lives and not to remain at the level of the text or language. However, postmodern feminists claim that to discuss the representation of women *is* to discuss the real. To show for example, how women are represented (constructed) in language is a seriously political act. On the other hand, the modernist feminist attempt to reify the category of woman into an artificial unity is more an authoritarian act than a politically emancipatory one; it merely camouflages contradictions and complexities. All in all, for postmodern feminists perhaps the most responsible political act is to expose – indeed *flaunt* those contradictions and complexities.

## *Is there a gulf?*

> Clustered tightly around the problem of the subject are the twin-terms of power and knowledge.
>
> (Rabinow, 1991: 12)

This idea of 'clustering' brings us back to the maypole image I introduced earlier. It reminds us that it is difficult if not impossible to think about these three things as independent from one another. From the discussion in this chapter it appears that modernist feminists and postmodern feminists do have rather different ideas and beliefs about each of these three things. For the modernist, politics is frequently understood as being about power and who gets 'what, when and where'. In order to make 'who gets what, when and where' fair and just, modernists claim that we need to establish correct and true principles and know precisely what these are (epistemology) and who they might be applied to (subjects). In order to do that, modernists have traditionally attempted to separate subjects or 'knowers' from the 'known' and to produce objective knowledge. Postmodernists are extremely sceptical about the possibility of any of this and prefer instead to ask how the 'who, what and where' come into being. Additionally they investigate what counts as fair and just principles, as well as the presumed separation between 'subjects' and 'objects'. This all leads to differing views about what counts as the most appropriate way to 'do politics'. Does this amount to a 'gulf' between these two broad streams of feminist thought?

Before addressing that question explicitly, I want to review the way I have written about feminist theory in these two chapters. In Chapter 1 I divided the feminisms into four blocs; liberal, radical, socialist and postmodern. In this chapter I have divided them into two blocs: modernist (comprising liberal, radical and socialist) and postmodernist. In Chapter 1 I explained and illustrated the many differences between the three modernist feminisms, and so, an important question must be: What is it that ties these three feminisms together under the label 'modernist'? In the epistemological arena it is very much the case that liberal and socialist feminists share the same ground. Both are rooted in a modernist epistemology that accepts Enlightenment concepts of a rationality that is flawed only by its sexism (Hekman, 1992: 40). Additionally, this epistemology informs, indeed structures, the political practices of liberal and socialist feminisms. For liberals this has typically meant political campaigns to have women included in the 'rational worlds of men'. On the other hand, socialist feminists have inherited and worked with the modernist epistemology of Karl Marx. This has implied that 'they accept not only the rational/irrational dichotomy so central to that epistemology, but also the modernist search for truth and liberation' (ibid.: 40). One might even claim that socialist feminists, especially in their earlier manifestations, are the quintessential modernists, because Marx's project was in many ways an attempt to complete the Enlightenment project that liberalism had failed to achieve (ibid.).

What about radical feminism? Typically, radical feminism rejects many of the fundamental principles of liberalism and Marxism, exalting non-traditional ways of accruing and thinking about knowledge. Often these would be ways that are classically associated with the 'feminine', for example, intuition. This may seem very much at odds with the feminisms influenced by liberalism and Marxism, but there is still an acceptance of the 'rational/irrational' dualism. Radical feminists may define women as 'less rational' than men, but this is seen, by them, as a 'good thing'. Additionally, there lurks a belief in a 'real female nature', which is distorted by patriarchy, as well as a desire to reach the truth, both about women's true needs and desires as well as the workings of patriarchy. These views about subjects and epistemology do appear to position radical feminism, in significant ways, within the modernist camp.

On the other hand, feminisms influenced by postmodernism fundamentally reject those feminisms typically associated with the 1970s as being shot through with the 'modernist impulse' (Barrett and Phillips, 1992: 2). They draw a sharp contrast – which Barrett and Phillips define as a gulf – between modernist 1970s feminisms and the feminisms more typical of the 1990s. The diversity of answers to the questions about women's disadvantaged position in society (misogyny? mistakes? class bias?) merely camouflaged the level of fundamental agreement between these feminisms. These agreements include a normative commitment to women's emancipation (or equality in the case of liberal feminism), a social scientific commitment to the explanation of women's oppression (or inequality), and a practical commitment to social transformation (McClure, 1992: 349). Each of the modernist feminisms identifies features (gender roles or patriarchy or alienation, for example) that were amenable to causal explanation and consequent instrumental manipulation. The purpose of theory for liberals, radicals and socialists is generally seen to offer both an explanation and suggestions for political action. In this sense, what unified modernist feminist theories was the normative commitment to identify, explain and end women's oppression/inequality.

Postmodern feminists argue that the modernist feminist project of striving for a unified, coherent, universally useful theory based on identity politics is misconceived. Postmodern feminists question all the concepts readily used by 1970s feminists including, 'causes', 'theory' and 'women's oppression'. They dispute the project of searching for causes, the claim that there is a cause or causes which can be discovered and used for explanatory purposes. Instead of asking 'why?', postmoderns prefer to ask 'how?' Modernist feminists have conceived theory as an explanatory tool and guide to action, while for postmoderns, theory is a method to expose the process of knowledge-making. Women's oppression, a phrase so often used by radical and socialist feminists in particular, has been problematised in two ways. First, the assumption is questioned that oppression can be identified objectively; and second, it is questioned whether all women, everywhere, were oppressed. Debates about 'women's oppression' generated a plethora of debates about essentialism, racism and ethnocentrism; these invoked such questions as 'Who is this "we" white woman?' and 'Who is woman, what is woman, how is woman?' As such, one of the aims of postmodern feminist theory is to destabilise the assumptions of modernist feminisms, especially as the latter have been said to be 'virtually useless' and 'anachronistic'.

### Does all this therefore add up to evidence of a gulf between modernist and postmodernist feminisms?

From the discussion here the answer must be 'yes'. It appears that the metatheoretical commitments of modernist and postmodernist feminisms are radically different. Modernism's commitment to certain epistemological foundations, the distinction between subject and object, the value and necessity of social scientific methods, and the explanatory and practical purpose of theory fundamentally structures the way modernist feminists understand and approach issues of gender, women and the feminine/female. These commitments lead to beliefs about the nature of the 'political' and the 'subject' which further structure how each of these theories understand the world. One of the aims of this book is to draw out the articulated and unarticulated assumptions and beliefs that underpin and structure different feminist theories, in order to discuss their political possibilities.

**Where to now?**

At the beginning of this chapter I suggested that the issue of a gulf between feminisms matters because so many of us seem to be involved in the search for an answer to the question, 'In the face of what is, what should we do?' (Price, 1997: 34). If feminist theories are importantly related to practice, then it probably matters that the theories are different. In the next two chapters I shall examine how these differing ways of doing and understanding feminist theory impact upon the realm of practice. This will provide a way to examine the very idea that there is a gulf at all.

**Note**

1  The work of Nietzsche is generally regarded as having a significant influence on postmodernist and poststructural thinking (1961, 1964, 1984).

# 3 Modernist feminisms and reproductive technologies

## Thinking theory through practice

[It is desirable to revitalise] the original agenda of second-wave feminism as committed to the practical liberation of women.

(Oakley, 1998: 133)

What is the modernist feminist story about reproductive technologies? How do feminist theories inspired by the ideas and values of modernism help us to think about the practices and implications of reproductive technologies? How will a discussion of these questions assist in examining the idea that there is a gulf between modernist and postmodernist feminisms? In this chapter I shall be evaluating some of the practices and processes of reproductive technologies as a way to examine the connections between theory and practice. Part of my reason for doing this is to explain more fully and more clearly what it means to say that there is a gulf between modernist and postmodernist feminisms. This will shed light on how feminist theories help us to 'know what to do' in everyday situations. In this chapter I want to return to the question I raised in the previous chapter, namely, 'In the face of what is, what should we do?' (Price, 1997: 34). If feminist theories are significantly different to each other, as the concept of a gulf implies, then this may inspire different answers or ways to approach the question of 'What should we do?'

In this chapter and the next, I want to look at an everyday practice and think about it through the three main categories I used in Chapter 2 – the subject, epistemology and politics. The set of practices I shall be looking at are reproductive technologies. My use of these technologies will be eclectic as I am not trying to provide an overall or universal explanation of them. I want to think about some of the uses of reproductive technologies through these varying feminist theories to see if we can think about them differently and, if so, whether this will help us know 'what we should do'. One might imagine that not all women would personally experience reproductive technologies. However, as these technologies can include anything that interferes with or is involved in the process of human reproduction (Stanworth, 1987: 10) or its prevention, and as such will include all forms of contraception as well as the most recent cloning and conceptive techniques, most women will have experiences of reproductive technologies at some point in their lives. Additionally, for those women who do become involved with reproductive technologies such as IVF or prenatal screening, it can become a big part of their everyday lives. Furthermore, and perhaps more significantly, the impact of shifting ideas and values (about human life and the integrity of the body for example) created by the use of reproductive technologies can affect all women in some way, regardless of their personal experience of such technologies. The central pragmatic point in the context of this chapter is to use a specific practical example in order to help us think about the differences between feminist theories. How, then, can we think about the subject in the context of reproductive technologies from modernist feminist perspectives?

## The subject

> There is such a thing as woman.
>
> (Bell and Klein, 1996: xix)

This assertion from Bell and Klein that 'there is such a thing as woman' gives us a pretty good idea of the answer to the question 'Which subject are modernist feminists primarily interested in?' Of course, in the generic context of reproductive technologies a number of subjects might be considered, for example; the woman, the foetus, the father and the doctor/physician/gynaecologist. But as we know from the discussions in the previous two chapters, the concept of the subject is very important to modernist feminists largely because of its perceived potential to allow the possibility of rational and autonomous decision-making (at the very least). This, together with the explicit political agenda of modernist feminisms to improve the status, role and indeed subject-hood of women in contemporary societies, implies that the primary subject to consider is indeed *woman*.

**Woman: a certain subject**

If we recall from the previous two chapters, modernist feminists are basically frightened of not being allowed to have control over their lives. The sexist and misogynist legacy of keeping women 'under control' (or attempting to) has propelled modernist feminists towards a desire to make sure the subject of woman has clear (human) foundations from which appropriate and recognised demands can be made. They hope for a sure, certain and recognisable subject. We might call this a vision of 'mature subjectivity', invoking an image of a reasoning, rational and authoritative adult – someone who is a competent and accountable decision-maker. This is all part of a claim to identity politics, as discussed in Chapter 1. How might we think about these claims to certain and mature subject-hood in the context of the practices and processes of reproductive technologies? As a way to start thinking about feminist theories and the practices of reproductive technologies, let me introduce three images invoked by their use.

*Image 3.1*

> *For the Hortons and an estimated one million other couples in Britain striving to overcome childlessness, doctors can now resort to a remarkable and increasing number of treatments. Advances in the use of drugs, surgical techniques and in vitro fertilisation mean that babies are now being born to couples who until quite recently would have been described as hopeless cases.*
>
> *(Prentice,* The Sunday Times, *1986: 10;*
> *quoted in Franklin, 1997: 89–90)*

*Image 3.2*

> *The [prenatal screening] tests permit parents who know they are at risk of bearing a defective baby to conceive, assured that if the test is positive, they can abort and try again for a healthy baby . . . It is heartless to deny parents access to medical technology that permits them to avoid giving birth to an incurably ill or severely retarded infant.*
>
> *(Rushing and Onorato, 1989: 273)*

*Image 3.3*

> *Reproductive technology concerns itself with the control and manip-*
> *ulation of women's bodies; it is based on an ideological assumption*
> *that woman equals [inefficient nature] and that male medicine can*
> *do it better. It constantly fragments and dismembers women during*
> *this process and it uses women as experimental subjects without*
> *obtaining their educated consent.*
>
> *(Rowland, 1992: 215)*

How do these three images make us think about reproductive technologies? Image 3.1 conjures up traditional ideas about the wonders
of modern science and medicine. Words like 'remarkable' and
'advances', alongside the image of previously 'hopeless' cases 'striving'
to 'overcome childlessness', lead us to think that there could not possibly be anything sinister or unpleasant or unhelpful about these reproductive technologies. How could helping women to have babies when
they otherwise would not do so but wish to be anything but good?
Or how could techniques such as ultrasound or amniocentesis, which
give the mother more information than she could ever have had previously, be problematic? Surely, as it is suggested in Image 3.2, it
would be cold and heartless to deny women access to these technologies
and the information they provide? However, Image 3.3 presents a very
different picture. This time reproductive technologies are described as
harmful to women in a number of ways – controlling them, fragment-
ing them, dismembering and experimenting on them. This all sounds
very sinister. Can we really believe this?

### Women: choosing subjects?

This idea of women being fragmented and dismembered by the use of
reproductive technologies seems quite opposed to the modernist
feminist desire for mature subjectivity for women. In the context of
contemporary reproductive technologies liberal feminism, for example,
appears to have achieved many of its goals in the arenas of choice,
rights and freedoms. For example, having more information about
one's foetus via ultrasound and amniocentesis; having a choice to
give birth to a baby despite infertility; having the right to make
decisions about giving birth to an abnormal or handicapped child.
All of these choices and decisions have to be made by someone considered and expected to be a rational and mature subject – someone
who is logically responsible for the consequences.

Of course, liberal feminists are acutely aware that the institutions of science and medicine have been both sexist and misogynist. For example, research has shown that many doctors' diagnoses of women's medical problems, and their ability to understand and make decisions about those problems, are based not on scientific facts about women's physiology, psychology, biology and anatomy, but on subjective assertions about women's 'natural' drives and 'natural' roles. Many medical textbooks contain some highly dubious assertions about women. This example comes from a 1971 text: 'the traits that compose the core of female are feminine narcissism, masochism and passivity' (cited in Foster, 1989: 338). Additionally, women are often pushed into passive roles when decisions have to be made. It has been regularly demonstrated that when women challenge doctors' judgements and take an assertive part in their healthcare, they are often regarded with contempt. One such hospital patient noticed, for example, that 'Watch this girl she is a know-it-all' had been written across the top of her medical notes in red (Foster, 1989: 340).

Many feminists have traced and exposed the history of sexism in these institutions and insist that such behaviours and expectations should be eradicated during the everyday practice of reproductive technologies. But despite the legacy of sexism and misogyny, all these new choices surely allow women more control over their lives than previously available. Choosing when and where to have children, even having a choice over the kind of child one has – normal and healthy as opposed to abnormal or unhealthy – must offer more control and equality for women, however unpleasant that last choice might appear. This might be perceived as relieving some of the burden that having children has entailed in the lives of women, especially when compared to the lives of men. How can we think about all of this in the context of modernist feminists striving for mature and certain subjectivity?

It is at this point that a significant difference between feminism informed by liberalism and feminisms of a more socialist and radical persuasion becomes apparent. The reliance on ideas about individuals being essentially separate (individualistic ontologies) inherent in liberalism inhibits liberal feminism from seriously considering, or indeed understanding, the impact of structures on women's lives. Conversely, socialist and radical feminists are very concerned with the significant impact that the structures of capitalism and patriarchy have on women's ability to become the mature subjects of modernism. It might *appear* that women's choices and freedoms have been increased by the proliferation of reproductive technologies. But perhaps this benign portrayal of what happens masks the reality. For radical and socialist feminists this masking or misrepresentation of the truth is a common occurrence in women's lives. Recall some of the examples I used in Chapter 1 about re-describing women's lives: domestic violence was one example; dieting might be another. Countless western women undernourish themselves in the pursuit of cultural norms of appropriate body weight. This is usually presented as a very personal decision made to correct greedy habits! A radical feminist would probably argue that the reality is that this is simply another patriarchal violence encouraging/forcing women to make themselves suffer for a goal which is totally 'man-made'!

So what is the socialist and radical feminist 'truth' about reproductive technologies? Is it as described in Image 3.3? If we recall from Chapter 1, I used the word 'control' as a relevant concept for both liberal and radical feminisms. Both groups of feminists prefer to have more control over their lives (as would all feminists presumably), but the concept of control implies more for radical feminists than this. For them it is also crucially about the level of control wielded *over* women's lives and their ability to make free decisions because of their position within patriarchy. Again recalling my introduction to radical feminism from Chapter 1, the point is to tell a different story to the mainstream or traditional one. It is only by re-describing reality (or that which appears to be reality) that the truth of women's experiences within patriarchy can be revealed.

The description in Image 3.3 certainly tells an alternative story. It tells the story of 'manipulated and controlled' bodies and of the representation of women's bodies as 'inefficient' while at the same time experimenting on them. The image of fragmentation and dismemberment is an evocative one, suggesting that pain is experienced by women during these processes. This is a powerful re-description as it depicts women as subjects in pain as a result of the uses of reproductive technologies – rather than subjects on their way to certain and mature subjectivity.

### Women: subjects in pain

The new reproductive technologies represent an escalation of violence against women, a violence camouflaged behind medical terms.

(Corea, 1990: 85)

What is the pain and the violence instigated by the use of reproductive technologies? For many radical feminists, women have always been measured and judged within patriarchy by their capacity to procreate. At times in history this has taken very sinister turns. For example, when slavery was more commonplace, black women were considered to be like animals from whom their babies could be sold 'like calves from a cow' (Corea, 1988: 272). These women were simply and cruelly used as breeders. Another example comes from the Nazi regime as the Third Reich had a plan to use women as reproductive prostitutes. In their attempt to 'purify' the German race, the Nazis developed a two-part programme: extermination and planned reproduction. Of course, these can be read as extreme examples which have no place in the twenty-first century. But if we consider that radical feminists believe that a continuum of abuse to women within patriarchy can be traced (not all of which will be as bad as the examples I have just cited), then it might be possible to start understanding how contemporary reproductive technologies could be abusive to women. Consider the example of IVF, which in Image 3.1 is depicted as a 'remarkable' procedure through which women can overcome their previously 'hopeless' childlessness and have a baby. Where is the pain here?

IVF is often presented as a simple, even natural procedure both by the clinics that carry out the procedure and in popular media reports (Franklin, 1997: 103). Simple images of egg removal, in vitro fertilisation in a dish with sperm and then reimplantation of the embryo popularly captured by the image of 'test-tube babies', have tended to give the impression of a miraculous but easy procedure which gives 'nature a helping hand' (ibid.). However, women who have undergone this procedure often paint a rather different picture. They tell of an exhausting and even 'assaultive' process which 'takes over their lives' (Rowland, 1992: 19; Franklin, 1997: 101). Consider the drugs involved in the process. In order to ensure that the best chance of conception is possible, women are given a cocktail of drugs to make them 'superovulate'. This means that the woman's body is made to produce more than the normal one egg per cycle (Rowland, 1992: 22). These drugs are largely powerful drugs which can have serious 'side-effects'.

A specific drug used in IVF, clomiphene citrate, is particularly problematic. The scientific literature on this drug suggests that there is a link with the development of cancer in women and the causation of abnormalities in children (ibid.: 50–51). Additionally it has other adverse effects 'including enlargement of ovaries, and in some cases [it] contributes to fertility problems by adversely affecting the post-ovulatory phase of a woman's menstrual cycle' (Spallone, 1989: 58).

It is believed that some of the drugs being used in IVF programmes are chemically related to known carcinogens. Moreover fertility drugs are associated with high rates of miscarriage. But the possible risks to women of ovarian cysts and other damage to the ovaries and menstrual cycle from IVF manipulation are infrequently mentioned by IVF practitioners (ibid.: 59). Examples of these other powerful fertility drugs are Clomid and Perganol, which have caused multiple pregnancies, hyperstimulation of the ovaries and ovarian cysts, and an increased incidence of cancer (Raymond, 1993: 12–13).

The drugs used and the procedure itself can clearly cause much pain and suffering to the women who undergo it. Even if the treatment is successful (one that ends with a live birth), there is more chance of a Caesarean section and multiple births, both of which run higher health risks for both mother and the child/ren. Additionally the risk of miscarriage, ectopic pregnancy, breech birth and stillbirth are all much higher with IVF (Greer, 1999: 81). But the pain is not just manifested physically. IVF has a very low success rate. The figures vary but in general the 'take-home baby rate' is between about 10 and 20 per cent (Franklin, 1997: 107; Greer, 1999: 81). This is a very low rate, especially considering the invasive nature of many of the procedures, the health risks involved but also, crucially, the emotional and psychological investment and pain experienced by the women 'who fail'. Consider these statements from women who have undergone IVF.

> It's a very intense procedure . . . you are being monitored all the time . . . and you do get very involved . . . it does take over your life to quite a big extent.
>
> (Franklin, 1997: 106)

> And you think the first time, oh yes, it's going to work . . . and the reason the disappointment is stronger than you'd expect is because it's like a set of hurdles, and each one that you're successful you build your hope a bit more.
>
> (Franklin, 1997: 107)

> When I was told after the third attempt that my eggs weren't good enough and that I should give up I was shocked and utterly devastated. I remained deeply depressed for more than a year and I was suicidal a lot of the time. I felt such an abysmal failure, a barren woman unable to give my husband a child and my parents their grandchild. I had even failed technology.
>
> (Rowland, 1992: 77)

The first two statements start to give an idea of how much women have to invest in the whole process in many ways in terms of time, hope and, no doubt, financially. Many women describe their experience with IVF as it becoming a 'way of life' (Franklin, 1997: 102). And if something becomes so much part of your life and so much is invested in it, 'failure' will hit hard. The third statement shows just how hard. And consider how the woman who made that statement interprets the failure – literally as hers. Not only does she think she has failed herself, her husband and her parents – but significantly she has 'failed' an inanimate 'thing' – technology. What does it mean when a woman believes she has failed technology?

It might be tempting to think that these latter stories about reproductive technologies and Image 3.3 are either extreme or rare. Perhaps it's just a few women who feel this way? Perhaps a certain amount of pain is to be expected in medical treatments of this nature? And what about the women who don't complain? What about the women who are successful?

For radical and socialist feminists, these questions miss the point in a big way. They suggest that the institutions of science and medicine and the technologies they produce are neutral and free (or potentially free) from the structures of capitalism and patriarchy. But radical and socialist feminists argue that all institutions are structured by capitalism and patriarchy; science and medicine are certainly not exempt. Moreover, women have specific places, roles and functions within these structures, which will necessarily create institutions and practices geared towards fulfilling these roles. This is not to say that all women have no choice but to 'serve their function', as it were, or that all actions are predetermined. If the structures worked so well, no one would be able to see them or fight against them. But it is often hard to make them visible, to do this reality has to be re-described in the ways that radical and socialist feminists do. To explain this more clearly, I want to introduce a fourth image.

### Women: useful subjects?

*Image 3.4*

> *The female body's generative capacity has now been discovered as a new 'area of investment' and profit-making for scientists, medical engineers and entrepreneurs in a situation where other areas of investment are no longer promising. Reproductive technologies have been developed not because women need them, but because*

> *capital and science need women for the continuation of their model of*
> *growth and progress.*
>
> *(Mies, 1993: 174–175)*

One of the driving forces of capitalism is profit. Existing sources of profit have to be thoroughly and efficiently used. New sources of profit constantly have to be created. The description in Image 3.4 strongly suggests that a new site of investment and profit-making is the female (re)productive body. How does this work?

Medical technology is big business. For example, in the mid-1990s the market for real-time ultrasound technology was in the region of $1 billion. But capitalism is not simply about making profits *per se*. The ideology of capitalism encourages a particular relationship to people which is geared towards getting the best use out of them in the context of satisfying the needs and ends of capitalism. Intertwined with patriarchal ideologies this can result in an attitude towards women which is not really in their best interests, according to socialist and radical feminists.

Take the specific example of prenatal screening technologies. As mentioned earlier, the manufacture and selling of these technologies are useful to capitalism. But what is prenatal screening for? What effects does its have? The usual medical story is that it gives women more information about their unborn babies. They can check for the health and/or normality of the foetus and if an abnormality is found, the mother is in a position to make a choice about 'what to do'.

In practice prenatal screening technologies are primarily used to detect abnormalities in the foetus and the result is often an abortion.

> The purpose of prenatal diagnosis is the recognition of a specific
> fetal abnormality . . . [I]n the great majority of cases early prenatal
> diagnosis is undertaken with a view to detecting fetal abnormalities
> sufficiently severe to justify termination under the UK's Abortion
> Act 1967.
>
> (Crawfurd, 1992: 755)

> The objective of screening is to identify fetal abnormalities.
>
> (Gilmore and Aitken, 1989: 22)

The decision to have an abortion in these circumstances may seem like an individual and freely chosen one. But, as we know, socialist and radical feminists tell a different story. One story they tell about prenatal screening is that it encourages (even forces?) women to carry out the eugenic needs of the state. Eugenics is concerned with creating the conditions under which 'fit and healthy' human beings will be born. However, what counts as 'fit and healthy' is not straightforward. The ideology of eugenics which promoted ideas about what counted as 'fit and healthy' and, by implication, who should be allowed to have children or to survive, has historically been very popular, particularly in the early part of the twentieth century in the US and Britain. One clearly devastating result of eugenic ideology was evident in Nazi Germany in the 1930s and 1940s, when many 'mental defectives' were sterilised. Many of the justifications for these sterilisations were grounded in economics. School children under the Nazi regime were given maths problems which asked them to work out the financial gain to the state of looking after 'mental defectives' in institutions compared to their not being alive at all.

The example of the Nazi extermination campaigns may seem to be another extreme example. What does this have to do with contemporary reproductive technologies? Radical and socialist feminists could argue that the ideology of eugenics is an extremely useful tool in the context of fulfilling economic needs. And that perhaps the ideology of 'reproducing the fittest' underpins prenatal screening technologies. As Stanworth pointed out, 'For much of this century, reproductive technologies have been seen by some as tools for reducing the numbers of the hereditarily unfit' (1987: 28).

There have been massive increases in genetic knowledge in the twentieth century. This has gone alongside a revival of interest in the biological bases of human behaviour. The media regularly bombard us with 'discovery stories' about a 'gay' gene or a 'criminal' gene, or an 'alcoholic' gene and so on. The scientific drive to find a 'one, true cause' of behaviours deemed problematic is a persistent one. Getting rid of 'problematic' children (who will grow into even more 'problematic' adults) before they are born can save the state a great deal of money. Putting forward such overt eugenic and socially engineering ideas is, though, not very popular today. However, some feminists claim that the ideology of 'search and destroy' lies at the base of prenatal screening technologies. Many women feel pressured into having an abortion if their foetus is found to be defective in some way: 'I had a choice in that no one would have forced me to have it, but psychologically I did not have any choice, in that if I hadn't had it I couldn't have gone through with the pregnancy' (Farrant, 1985: 111).

Many women clearly want to have an abortion if they realise they will give birth to a handicapped child. But just because they make such a choice does not mean that this choice is freely made. One might even argue that the structures and ideologies of patriarchy and capitalism have engineered a rather clever way of using women's bodies to ensure 'healthy' offspring. 'Prenatal diagnosis . . . forces women to fulfil their eugenic duty' (Degener, 1990: 89). Women not only have to go through the physical and emotional trauma of the abortion, but they also have to take the responsibility for making the decision – as any 'mature and accountable subject' of the modern era might be expected to.

## Which subjects matter?

These alternative stories about reproductive technologies should give us cause to think again about the role and nature of the subject of woman in the context of reproductive technologies. The vision of the choosing and accountable subject seems to sit uneasily alongside the structures and ideologies of capitalism and patriarchy. What emerges is a clash of stories whereby on the one hand IVF and prenatal screening are largely presented by the medical establishment and the popular press as examples of advances in modern science and medicine designed to help women with certain reproductive choices. Women undergoing them are presented as rational, choosing and accountable adults (as any self-respecting liberal feminist would desire). But when radical and socialist feminists tell the other stories, we get visions of coerced and abused women, as Image 3.5 below depicts.

*Image 3.5*

> *[We should] resist the development and application of these technologies globally, in the interests of all women, in the knowledge that these technologies are harmful to women, a destruction of women's physical integrity, an exploitation of women's procreativity and yet another attempt to undermine women's struggle for control of our own reproduction.*
>
> *(Spallone, 1989: 1)*

This image of women being exploited might mean that women do not matter as much as feminists think they should. Or at least that as subjects, the clash of their interests with larger interests (capitalism, patriarchy, scientific advances) weakens the circumstances in which women can be fully autonomous. If we think about the central influences of two of the main modernist feminist theories – liberalism and Marxism – these theories were largely written by men and based on men's lives. But as radical feminists consistently point out, women's lives are very often different to men's. It is still the case, in this new century, that only women can give birth (though for how long I do not know). Additionally, the science that underpins reproductive technological advances has developed within structures of capitalism and patriarchy and therefore all the scientific explanations and justifications are likely to result in mixed if not dubious results in the context of women's lives.

Numerous stories can be told about reproductive technologies in the context of the subject. This might lead us to want an answer to the question 'Which is the true story?' As I explained in Chapter 2, we really need to think of the three themes of the subject, epistemology and politics in terms of a maypole – all deeply intertwined. Asking 'Which is the true story?' takes us right into the realm of what we use to construct the truth and that is knowledge (epistemology).

## Epistemology

### *How do subjects know?*

If we recall the discussion about epistemology from Chapter 2, searching out and proving the truth is very important for modernist feminists. This is largely because discovering the objective truth is a way to distinguish truth from prejudice and lies and should ensure that people are treated fairly and justly. All modernist feminists believe that there have been many false stories about women which have been presented as the truth. This has been the case particularly when women have behaved in 'inappropriate' ways. Think of the example of the vilification of the suffragettes for demanding the right to vote. They were frequently depicted as nagging, ugly old women! Modernist feminists have traditionally worked for the 'truth to come out'. What is the truth about reproductive technologies and how can women know or find the truth?

Once again, liberal feminists depart from radical and socialist feminists on how to think about these issues and questions. For liberals, there has been a strong tendency to accept the inherent epistemological neutrality of institutions and practices such as medicine, science and technology. Of course, we know about the misogynist and sexist legacy, but for liberals this can ultimately be ameliorated. However, both radical and socialist feminists believe that the truth very much depends on who has the power to represent it – therefore they work with ideas about the *socially constructed* nature of the truth. Alongside this, they believe that knowledge and the institutions that deliver knowledge (such as science and medicine) are contaminated and constructed by unpleasant and debilitating ideologies, for example patriarchy and capitalism. In simple terms, the knowledge that these institutions purvey will reflect and reinforce the interests, needs, drives and desires of those huge structural ideologies, resulting in the production of biased knowledge. What use is a mature and accountable subject when institutional knowledges and practices are so biased?

### How do 'different' subjects' know?

As we know from Chapter 2, the traditional and authoritative 'knowing subject' of modernism has been man. Women have traditionally been seen as less than authoritative and respectable knowers. But it is one thing to say that women have been *treated* as less than authoritative knowers and quite another to say that women *are*, not less authoritative knowers, but *different* knowers to men. Let me go back to one of the earlier examples in which it was argued that women are forced to fulfil their eugenic duty by aborting abnormal foetuses. Imagine the scenario. A woman finds out that she is carrying an abnormal foetus – perhaps one with Down's Syndrome, which is a condition easily detected with prenatal diagnosis. Of course, not all women will make the decision to abort. This will depend on a number of things for example, her religious beliefs, whether she already has a child with a handicap, and whether she lives in a supportive environment. But there is much evidence to suggest that many women feel pressured to abort: after all, if prenatal screening services were to result in no or very few abortions, the cost in financial terms would be prohibitive. In this sense, prenatal screening is ultimately based on the assumption that most women will make the decision to abort.

What epistemological questions might we ask here? Let us start with one about the competence of women to make rational and authoritative decisions. The model of decision-making in the context of such a reproductive choice seems relatively simple – even common-sensical. A human adult (a 'mature subject') faced with a difficult decision has to weigh up the pros and cons and make a judgement. It is not implied that it is an easy decision, but this rational, liberal model of decision-making has a history and a context. There is an emphasis on having as much information as possible and on having a clear understanding of and access to one's own desires and interests. But perhaps this model assumes the presence – the ontological reality – of a single decision-maker who has the 'psychological capacity and authority to make a coherent, single decision' (Gregg, 1995: 15). Maybe this is not the case for women undergoing prenatal screening.

Alarm bells may be going off for some of you at this point. Am I suggesting that women are incompetent decision-makers and as such reinforcing stereotypical views of the 'pathetic feminine woman'? Well – the answer is yes and no! No, I am not saying women are incapable or incompetent. However, if we consider that judgements and *knowledges* about what counts as incapable and incompetent are caught up in the web of patriarchal and capitalist ideas, this might make us stop and reconsider what it means to be incompetent and incapable.

### Free-floating individuals?

The very notion of individuals being essentially separate is called into question by the experience and nature of pregnancy. Two hearts, two minds, two souls, two bodies; all within and around the one. If contemporary western models of decision-making are based on philosophies and social theories and practices centring on men's lives, it is not surprising that such an individualistic and masculinist model of rational decision-making has emerged as the measure of competency and capability (Grimshaw, 1986: 165–176). It is also not surprising that this model may be inappropriate for women, especially in the context of pregnancy and making decisions to abort, and particularly in a situation in which the pregnancy is a planned and wanted one.

One of the reasons this may be inappropriate for women generally, according to some feminists, is that women undergo a different psychological development to men. Much of the work on the psychological differences between men and women comes from feminists particularly interested in standpoint epistemologies and the construction of differently valued epistemologies. The argument is not that women and men are inherently different, but that societal training makes them different. I introduced one classic study on this in Chapter 1 – that is the work of Carol Gilligan (1982) on models of gendered decision-making. Her initial 'inspiration' was the work of her former teacher Lawrence Kohlberg on justice and moral reasoning. Kohlberg developed a six-point scale by which to measure how advanced an individual's decision-making abilities were in the context of morality and justice. The higher up the scale, the more advanced one was. For Gilligan, there were two central problems with Kohlberg's work; one was that his research was based on boys and men and the second was that when girls and women were tested using his six-point scale, they rarely got past stage three. She argued that the point was not to try and prove that women and men were the same or made moral judgements in the same way. It was rather that the different ways in which women made judgements were not *valued* in the same ways. This brings us right back to the hierarchy of gender I introduced in Chapter 1 in the section on radical feminism. If women learn to be other than rational and autonomous thinkers in societies divided and constructed by gender, perhaps the valued masculinist and individualistic model of decision-making is both inappropriate and even unavailable to women, especially in circumstances of difficult reproductive decision-making.

However, despite the idea that women may be 'different knowers', it is difficult to live such a difference within the epistemological frameworks of capitalism and patriarchy. Women often end up in a whirl-pool of competing and conflicting ideologies and values – especially in the context of motherhood. Women are still generally expected to want to have children at some point in their lives and that their children will become a central and defining part of their lives. As we know, in the contemporary west this often conflicts with other ideas about what women should do, for example that they are willing and able to compete with men in the public world of work at the highest levels. It still remains difficult for a woman to be a full-time paid employee and a full-time mother. Guilt and exhaustion are but two consequences of this.

Guilt together with pain is a defining consequence of many reproductive decisions for women. Much of the feminist psychological and epistemological literature suggests that women develop a different sense of *self* than men – one that is more relational and linked in with caring about the well-being of others. This is again very different to the masculinist, autonomous rational model of decision-making to which the ideal 'mature subject of modernism' is meant to aspire and exemplify. The ideology of the caring, loving and selfless mother is a significant one. Yet women are expected to make decisions to abort foetuses that are found to be abnormal. Of course, many will feel bad about making these decisions – even if they think it is the right decision for them in the context of their own lives. The distress and conflict that women experience during the decision-making process have consistently been underplayed or simply ignored by the medical establishments that provide such services (Farrant, 1985: 109). This all adds weight to the suggestion that perhaps women 'don't matter' as much as some feminists would like them to. A flavour of the cycle of guilt and confusion comes through in the following quotation.

If a woman does not want the test [prenatal screening], this requires signing a form stating that the test is refused . . . If a woman refuses the test yet bears a child with some 'defect', she lays herself open to feelings of guilt that the child need not have been born 'defective'.

(Klein, 1990: 242–243)

## Scientific knowledges

I mentioned earlier that science and medicine are not immune from the ideologies of capitalism and patriarchy. What kinds of epistemological questions should this make us consider? Many feminists, especially radical and socialist feminists, argue that the historical and epistemological trajectory of any institution has to be analysed in order to achieve a better understanding of how women's lives have been affected by these institutions. Because science has been such a major influence over the past 200 years or so, this has been a central area to which feminists have looked for evidence of patriarchy and capitalism at work. Using the description in Image 3.4, I have already touched upon the ways in which the capitalist profit motive and need for healthy bodies to turn the wheels of capitalism play a part in providing a market for much of the equipment used in reproductive technologies and justifying the (ab)use of women's bodies in the process.

But science and the medicine and technology that emerge from it are not simply about physical forms – whether they be machines or medicines or human bodies. Science produces knowledge. And scientific knowledge helps produce how we think. If science is patriarchal, this will profoundly affect how women think about themselves and how women are thought about. This in turn will have major effects on women's real lives. Let us remind ourselves of Image 3.3.

> *Reproductive technology concerns itself with the control and manipulation of women's bodies; it is based on an ideological assumption that woman equals [inefficient nature] and that male medicine can do it better. It constantly fragments and dismembers women during this process and it uses women as experimental subjects without obtaining their educated consent.*
>
> *(Rowland, 1992: 215)*

## Scientifically fragmented and dismembered women?

What can feminist writers mean when they speak of 'fragmentation and dismemberment'? They clearly don't mean the literal/physical dismemberment of women's bodies. Instead, this image of the 'breaking up' of women's bodies is to do with how women think about themselves and how this affects their sense of self, together with how others think about women. Essentially the argument is that patriarchal and capitalist science and technology are driven in specific ways that produce knowledge and values that harm women, particularly in the context of reproduction. Let me explain this a little more.

In Chapter 1 I introduced the idea that many feminists believe that science is driven by the desire to conquer and control. For some feminists this masculinised need to control is linked in with a masculine envy of women's power to give birth. Through numerous customs and traditions, men have 'attempted to detract from the woman's importance and pretend to give birth themselves' (Corea, 1988: 285). This has included varied practices which redefine the 'birth' of children in ways that enable men to make a claim on them. Christian baptism is one example; another is biological theories (which held sway for a very long time), which claimed that women's contribution to the conception of a baby was minimal (Corea, 1988; O'Brien, 1981; Tuana, 1989). If we recall that many radical feminists fear for the future of women, one fear is that contemporary reproductive technologies offer not only ways to dismember and fragment women, but also ways to erase women (or their importance) altogether: 'The adequate androcratic invasion of the gynocentric realm can only be total erasure/elimination of female presence, which is replaced by male femininity' (Daly, 1979: 87).

### Scientifically erased women?

Of course, Daly's assertion can sound completely over the top. What can it mean? As mentioned earlier, modernist feminists of a radical and socialist persuasion are very concerned with the socially constructed nature of reality and human identity. Societies that are run on patriarchal and capitalist values will produce humans in accordance with the needs of those ideologies (although there is always resistance). In this context, the argument is that men have traditionally been envious of women's power to give birth and in the further context of a masculinist drive towards control, the knowledge and technologies that science has developed give men the possibility to consistently remove this power. As stated above, this has traditionally implied the construction of ideas, theories and practices that reduce the importance of the role of women in the whole process. However, there has also been the increasing possibility, literally, to take the power of birth away from women. This has both physical and epistemological effects – the two are inextricably linked.

Take the example of prenatal screening. According to some feminists, the increasing surveillance and monitoring of pregnancy that this has created alongside the increasing visibility of the foetus in the womb has had negative implications for women. Women may be prenatally screened for different reasons. Some will be defined as 'at risk' (of giving birth to an abnormal child), others will simply have blood tests and ultrasound as part of routine prenatal care. One of the consequences of all this monitoring has been to remove the locus of authoritative knowledge about 'what is happening' away from the woman and into the hands (and 'minds') of the medical establishment. It used to be the case that women would tell people that they were pregnant on the evidence of the changes in their own bodies (absence of menstruation, feeling the movement of the foetus, changing body shape). In the contemporary west, it would be highly unusual for a woman suspecting she was pregnant not to seek confirmation of this from the medical establishment. Apart from the gradual shifting of the locus of authoritative knowledge about what is happening inside the woman's body away from the woman, there is the linked effect of the changing experience of pregnancy and motherhood for women.

One example of this is the 'tentative pregnancy' syndrome (Katz-Rothman, 1988). This means that for many women in the contemporary west, family and friends are not told of the pregnancy until the 'all clear' has been given by the doctor (meaning that prenatal screening has declared the baby normal as far as can be ascertained). This all adds to the overall sense of fragmentation and dismemberment of the experience of pregnancy and motherhood for women. For many feminists this is part of a serious manipulation and abuse of the epistemological status and the subjectivities of women. I have already gestured towards the impact of the significance of 'where authoritative knowledge' lies. But there is perhaps an even more serious point to make and that is the alteration of the feelings, knowledges and senses of self (the cluster of things that make up subjectivity) this implies for women.

### Woman as machine?

The quantum leaps in technology in the twentieth century have provoked a profound shift in the way we think about our bodies.

> Genetic engineering, reproductive technology . . . all fundamentally
> affect basic categories of 'self'.
>
> (Stabile, 1994: back cover)

Machine technology has become a common feature in the monitoring
of pregnant women prenatally and during birth. Machines produce
images of the foetus in the womb and machines monitor the progress
of the labour and birth. How many of us have not seen an image of
the foetus in the womb – often resembling a little astronaut floating
in space? There are several implications to the increasing use of
machines in reproduction.

The first is that it creates new knowledge about what is inside the
pregnant woman's body. On this point let me introduce Image 3.6.

*Image 3.6*

> *These new technologies . . . help chip away at women's right to repro-*
> *ductive freedom . . . I contend that these technologies focus medical,*
> *legal, and media attention on the status of rights of fetuses and men*
> *while rendering the status and rights of women at best incidental and*
> *at worst invisible.*
>
> *(Raymond, 1990: 45)*

If it is the case that women don't matter as much as feminists think they
should, this should give us cause for concern about the increasing
visibility of the foetus. This is especially the case in the context of liberal
democracies, where there is a formal emphasis on individual rights.
If radical and socialist feminists argue that the theory and practice of
rights are built upon a masculinist legacy with an emphasis on ideas
about separate, autonomous individuals, then it comes as no surprise
that this jars with the duality of the pregnancy. Who is the individual –
the subject – in pregnancy? The woman, the foetus – perhaps even the
father? We might want to assume the primary individual and important
subject is the woman but in societies infused with the values and beliefs
of capitalism and patriarchy, this may not be the case.

This visual erasure of women assisted by technologies such as ultrasound can be used to 'isolate the embryo as astronaut, extraterrestrial,
or aquatic entity . . . [which has] enormous repressive reverberations in
the legal and medical management of women's bodies' (Stabile, 1994:
72). Think of the example of Angela Carder, a 28 year old white
woman, 26 weeks pregnant, who had received a terminal prognosis
for bone cancer and was ordered by the Washington court to undergo

a Caesarean section. Against Carder's explicit wishes, against the opinion of her attending physician, against the protests of her husband and parents, the doctors refused to prescribe chemotherapy because of its potential effects on the foetus. A Caesarean section was performed and, 'Carder barely lived long enough to hear that the fetus extracted from her uterus had died, if indeed it could be said to have lived at all' (ibid.).

### Fragmented subjects: body/mind parts

As we know, radical and socialist feminists generally believe in the socially and culturally constituted nature of reality. Unlike liberal feminists, radical and socialist feminists argue that what happens to the body, how the body is seen and understood, and how we feel within and about our bodies all play a vital part in constructing epistemological realities.

Over the last couple of centuries especially in the west, the technological, scientific and medical involvement in pregnancy and birth has increased dramatically. What used to be an occasion which took place in the home, usually involving female friends and relatives, has now become a highly monitored and technological event. For many feminists this has implied a reduction in the value of women's own knowledge about their pregnancies and their own control of them. This arguably has had the effect of further reducing the epistemological status of women and, by association, the feminine. For radical feminists especially, this marks a return to a belief in women as *less valued* knowers.

The increasing visualisation of the foetus through technologies such as ultrasound has, for many feminists, helped to displace the primary importance of the subject of woman towards the foetus. For socialist feminists in particular, this, combined with eugenic ideologies, has encouraged the use of technologies which can 'search out' foetuses that are not considered useful to society. States have consistently looked for ways to 'eliminate' the poor and disabled as a way to deal with poverty (Koval, 1987: 19). The increasing 'apparent' separation between the maternal body and the foetus can also prove very useful in the context of concerns about financial drains on the state. Some have described the separation of foetus and maternal body as a 'civil war within female bodies' (Stabile, 1994: 72). This civil war has 'proved a formidable weapon in the hands of the New Right' (ibid.: 91). The image of the foetus floating as if in space gives the impression that it exists in an environment where it miraculously receives shelter and food – diverting attention away from questions about the economic situation of pregnant women and their access to basic needs like food, shelter and healthcare. The increasing emphasis of foetal rights can appear benign, but

> in protecting this 'endangered species' the New Right can override and dismiss material needs of the female bodies that house these cosmonauts, as well as the needs of children and their families. While the fetus needs protection (a thinly disguised alibi for controlling women), it doesn't demand money.
>
> (Ibid.: 91)

Technologies such as IVF further place the knowledge and expertise regarding pregnancy and motherhood in the hands of science and 'medical men'. I mentioned earlier that men had traditionally created all sorts of practices to allow them to make a 'real' claim to the ownership of children. Many feminists would argue that this is happening again, whereby women owe the birth of their babies to the medical practitioners: 'Reproductive technologies do more than give males a sense of continuity over time. They are transforming the experience of motherhood and placing it under the control of men' (Corea, 1988: 289).

This idea of the dismembered and fragmented female body is reinforced by descriptions of women in medical literature, for example as 'uterine environments' (Rowland, 1992: 211). Radical feminists especially worry about how all this impacts upon women. Andrea Dworkin – our quintessential radical feminist – compares sexual prostitutes who sell 'vagina, rectum and mouth' with the emergence of 'reproductive prostitutes' who will sell other body parts, 'womb, ovaries, eggs' (Corea, 1988: 275). Who will be the pimps of the reproductive prostitutes?

Both physically and in terms of women's identity as mothers and epistemologically as female knowers, reproductive technologies are seen as a threat by radical feminists. And of course, this can be seen clearly with a specific use of prenatal screening technology – the literal erasure of females by the practice of female feticide.

In China, for example, it has become evident that the eradication of female foetuses is not uncommon (Warren, 1985). This is instigated by official limits on family size and the belief that female babies are less desirable than male babies, especially in rural areas. This sex preselection is having major repercussions on the sex ratio balance in both China and India. In 1901 in India there were 972 women per 1,000 men.

In 1981 there were 925 women per 1,000 men. The 'deficit' in women was 9 million in 1901 and 22 million in 1981 (Rowland, 1992: 85). In China only 100 girls are born for every 114 boys. This is resulting in a shortage of marriage-age women, especially in rural areas. As a result, a new thriving business for underworld gangs has been to abduct young women from cities and sell them as wives (*Newsweek*, 13 September 1993). In July 1993 Beijing police uncovered a gang that had sold more than 1,800 young women to villages in Shanxi province. It is perhaps not surprising that in China the highest suicide rate occurs among rural women aged 20 to 24. A report in the *Guardian* claimed that for a growing number of wives in China, having a baby girl vastly increased the risk of violence on the part of her husband, and the chance of divorce (16 November 1994). The author of the report, Debbie Taylor, records that one survey in China found that in a third of all divorces, having a daughter was the stated reason. On a visit to one mother, whose husband had divorced her because she had given birth to a daughter, the reporter asked the child, aged 5, whether she remembered her father. The child replied that 'He doesn't want Mother any more because I am a girl'. A very poignant example of how females don't matter as much as feminists would like them to.

## Politics

### What's a modernist feminist to do?

In the face of these stories about reproductive technologies, what do modernist feminists want to happen? This, of course, is a question about politics. If we recall the discussion about modernist feminist politics from Chapter 2, to 'do politics' generally implies having an agenda or a project commonly consisting of a 'wish list' of needs or wants and carrying out some sort of practical action to achieve concrete results. In this context, liberal, radical and socialist feminists are rather similar in the ideas they have about what 'doing politics' means – though some of the desired results may be quite different. One thing that all feminists appear to share is a recognition that there is a politics involved in the sexing or gendering of human beings. What this means is that they all believe that different societal benefits and burdens will follow dependent on what sex you are or are deemed to be. This has been perhaps most obvious in the realm of reproduction, which has historically been so overwhelmingly associated with women. This is a

site where politics around women's bodies and identities have traditionally and consistently been carried out.

The first thing for a modernist feminist, however, is to work out what
the 'problem is'. There is a general consensus that women have been
and are badly treated in some way because of their sex. The idea,
then, is to work out what form the bad treatment takes, what the
causes are (if at all possible), and then suggest or demand some
practical action that will hopefully ensure that a change takes place.
In the realm of reproductive technologies, there are at least two con-
texts for modernist feminists to consider: (a) the practice and usage
of reproductive technologies on women, and (b) the reasons for their
existence and the implications of that. If we accept that all feminists
would prefer that women be treated well and with respect and care,
then it is probably accurate to say that they are all interested in the
politics of non-sexist healthcare. For example, the following questions
might be asked in the context of amniocentesis.

> Who gets the test and under what conditions? What does informed
> consent mean and how can we expand and insure its use? How can
> women who opt for amniocentesis learn the social as well as the
> medical 'facts' of the diagnoses their fetuses receive? How can we
> make second trimester abortions less devastating for the women
> who choose them? How can we insure that accurate, up-to-date
> information about prenatal diagnosis, explained in clear, non-
> jargon language is available to women?
>
> (Rapp, 1985: 324–326)

Most feminists would approve of these sorts of questions in the context
of the practice of this reproductive technology, though radical and
socialist feminists might be sceptical of the possibility of truly adequate
responses to them. Truly good healthcare for women may not be
possible in institutions structured around other interests. Why, for
example, is women's anxiety in prenatal screening situations treated
as irrelevant simply because it is often transitory (Green, 1990: 13)?
Or why is it that the 'emotional implications of prenatal screening
are largely overlooked by the medical profession and by those involved
in the planning of services' (Farrant, 1985: 109)? However, it is within
the second context – why do these technologies exist and what are
the implications of their use? – that significant differences between
modernist feminists emerge. In order to discuss these differences in the
context of modernist feminist politics, let me introduce a final image.

*Image 3.7*

> *Mrs. M., suspecting pregnancy, engages the services of an attorney*
> *who specializes in family law, especially prenatal agreements. On*
> *her initial visit to the fetologist, Mrs. M. and her attorney will be*
> *informed of the conditions to which she must adhere throughout the*
> *pregnancy, and a second attorney will be appointed as fetal guardian.*
> *Violations of the prenatal contract will result in the state gaining*
> *custody of the fetus: either forcibly removing it to an artificial*
> *womb, or putting Mrs. M. in one of the new high-security wings of*
> *the maternity hospital for the duration of her pregnancy.*
>
> *(Rothman, 1989: 163)*

### Fear for the future

In the futuristic image above, it appears that women such as Mrs M. are
still giving birth, but under very restricted conditions. This may be an
imagined scenario, but for radically inspired feminists the point is to tell
different stories about the past, present *and* future in order that
women's lives can be better understood and concrete political action
taken to improve their lives. Under conditions of patriarchy and
capitalism the potential for further control over women's bodies and
lives is enormous, as Image 3.1 indicates. Not only might women
have less control over their pregnancies but the possibility of losing
the power of birth altogether is a fear many feminists share. This is
especially the case for radical feminists, as they generally believe that
men have a serious and consistent case of 'womb envy', or 'birth or
paturation envy dating back to Neolithic times' (Corea, 1985: 283).
What better way to ameliorate this than to take the power of birth
away from women. And as our 'quintessential' radical feminist asks,
'What will happen when men can make babies?' (Dworkin, 1983: 173).

In the Hollywood film *Junior*, Arnold Schwarzenegger becomes
'pregnant' and gives birth to a baby girl. This spectacle doesn't exactly
fill one with fear given the comedic absurdities of the 'Terminator' star
in a huge pink skirt suit and becoming 'all emotional'. But for many
feminists the potential and capacities for some reproductive technologies to remove and control women's power over birth imply
direct political action. Of course, the art of re-presenting the story of
'what is happening' is an important political practice. I have recounted
many of these stories earlier in this chapter but let me provide another
brief example here. Further evidence of the idea that perhaps females
don't matter as much as feminists would like them to is provided by

the use of prenatal sex determination techniques. If we think that one of the drives of masculinist science is to 'develop procedures to create "perfect" "unproblematic" people' (Rowland, 1992: 81) combined with the traditional patriarchal idea that women have less value than men, then getting rid of females even before they are born is a pretty convenient way of achieving this aim.

Amniocentesis is a prenatal test that will confirm the sex of the foetus. In India, although amniocentesis followed by abortion for sex determination was banned in public hospitals in 1975, private clinics do not fall under this legislation. One study in Bombay indicated that of 8,000 cases of abortion, 7,997 were female foetuses (ibid.: 84). One Indian woman responding to the question, 'Do you think it will have to continue like that?' (meaning testing and abortions again and again) replied,

> Yes, that's what I mean . . . but I shall do it if only my body will take it. And I am afraid that my husband will divorce me and take a new wife who will give him sons . . . you just don't know what I have been going through in the last seven years because all I gave birth to were girls . . . it would be so much easier for me with a son. My husband and his family would respect me so much more.
>
> (Ibid.: 81)

The general preference for male offspring is also a western phenomenon, as shown in a North American study. Here men and women who consider themselves sensitive to female inequality would still choose to have male babies if sex-predetermination technology were available to them (Spallone, 1989: 126). This would more than likely not involve selective abortion in the US at the present time but the preference for male babies is a cause of concern for feminists such as Spallone. For many radical feminists this re-telling of stories culminates in the idea that, 'the new reproductive technologies represent an escalation of violence against women, a violence camouflaged behind medical terms' (Corea, 1990: 85).

### Concrete action

To stem this violence one form of political action that radical feminists have taken is the formation of a cohesive political coalition in order to spread 'the word' about the dangers of new reproductive technologies and to take steps to halt their further advance. In March 1984 the Leeds

Reproductive Rights Group organised one of the first feminist confer-
ences in the world on new reproductive technologies (Corea, 1988: 327).
In the following month several of the women participating in that
conference went on to help found the Feminist International Network
on the New Reproductive Technologies (FINNRET) in Gronigen, the
Netherlands. In July 1985 a five-day Women's Emergency Conference
on the New Reproductive Technologies was held in Vallinge, Sweden,
with seventy-four women from sixteen countries. At this conference the
women changed FINNRET's name to the Feminist International
Network of Resistance to Reproductive and Genetic Engineering
(FINRRAGE), a name better reflecting the ideology of the network
(ibid.: 329). At this conference a resolution emerged to

> resist the development and application of these technologies glob-
> ally, in the interests of all women, in the knowledge that these tech-
> nologies are harmful to women, a destruction of women's physical
> integrity, an exploitation of women's procreativity and yet another
> attempt to undermine women's struggle for control of our own
> reproduction.
>
> (Spallone, 1989: 1)

The original group of seventy-four women from sixteen countries grew
to hundreds within a few years, forming an international network of
information-sharing and feminist resistance.

### Politics of choice and freedom

As we know, not all modernist feminists agree that reproductive
technologies represent an escalation of violence against women. For
feminists inspired by liberalism, reproductive technologies have actually provided more options for women and are therefore very much
implicated in a growing sense of freedom for women. Before reliable
contraception and safe legal abortion (at least in the west), women
were often at the mercy of unplanned and unwanted pregnancies and
too many children. Being stuck at home with children is not the best
way to have a great career in the public world. The ability to control
if and when one has children has been perceived as an enormously
important part of women's ability to become the mature and autonomous subjects of modernity. Reproductive rights campaigns have
been a vital part of many feminist agendas. For liberal feminists the
ability to have control in this area has been a sign of the progressive
nature of modernist values.

Of course, radical and socialist feminists are much more dubious about the 'truth' of the freedom and control that women have as a result of reproductive technologies. For example, the introduction of the contraceptive pill in the 1960s may have prevented unwanted pregnancies, but it also meant that women were ingesting large doses of hormones for three weeks each month without really knowing what the side-effects might be. Additionally, it meant that women might have less choice about saying no to sexual intercourse. The traditional 'excuse' of fearing pregnancy had suddenly become less convincing. For many radical feminists, the contraceptive pill was developed with men's needs in mind, since it emphasises the sexual enjoyment of men and underestimates the costs to women (Pollock, 1985: 76).

## What is the modernist feminist 'story' about reproductive technologies?

> In the face of what is, what should we do?
>
> (Price, 1997: 34)

I started this chapter by asking the question, 'What is the modernist feminist story about reproductive technologies?' As we have seen, those modernist feminists influenced by liberalism have a somewhat different story to tell about the practices, experiences and explanations of and for reproductive technologies than do radical or socialist feminists. So what is it that joins these three feminisms together? Are the similarities more important than the differences? And how can all this help towards addressing the issue of a gulf between modernist and postmodernist feminisms and how this impacts on the everyday? I shall conclude this chapter by summarising the differences and similarities amongst modernist feminisms on the three categories I have used for my discussion, namely the subject, epistemology and politics.

An initial political act that all modernist feminists carry out is the (ontological) one of placing the subject of woman towards (if not at) the centre of analysis and concern. All these feminists have argued that women have been unfairly treated and/or oppressed because of their sex and that one way to ameliorate this injustice is by insisting that women have more importance and value than they have traditionally been ascribed. Liberal feminists relying on traditional modernist ideas, values and methods have attempted to demonstrate that women are as valuable as men. They none the less recognise that there are some significant biological and physical differences between men and women – obviously manifested in the arena of reproduction –

but that this should not hinder women's participation in the public sphere. One way to achieve this, according to liberal feminists, is to ensure women have more choice about their lives. For this reason, liberal feminists have largely welcomed the 'advances' that reproductive technologies have ushered in. In this sense the sexual politics involved implied a move away from the restrictions of women's reproductive biology and towards the right to choose to have children or not, and of course to have the choice not to have particular kinds of children (those with disabilities for example).

Radicals and socialists claim that a politics of rights on behalf of women does not necessarily make women's lives better because the politics of rights can set up a battle over whose rights are paramount – the woman's, the foetus's or the father's? For some feminists, the issue of rights claims has been taken to an extreme if logical outcome, whereby the rights of 'ejaculatory fathers' are taken seriously over and above the rights of women (Raymond, 1990: 48).

Radical and socialist feminists believe that the capitalist and patriarchal structure of societies drastically mitigates the possibility of improving women's lives by placing them in the centre. While they share with liberal feminists the view that women have been undervalued, they disagree with liberal feminists that the solution is simply to move women into the centre that men have traditionally created and occupied. Radical and socialist feminists create a different centre – one where women's 'real' interests (those not tethered by the constraints of capitalism and patriarchy) are revealed and nurtured. Here, the truth of the emotional and physical pain women endure during many of the processes of reproductive technologies can be told. Additionally, the truth of the drives underpinning masculinist and patriarchal science and technology can be revealed, like their 'ultimate technological fantasy' of 'the creation without mother' (Huyssen, 1986: 70). As these examples illustrate, liberal feminists and radical and socialist feminists differ on how they revalue women and what it means to place women at the centre. Nevertheless, the subject of woman is a necessary point of departure for all modernist feminist identity politics.

Epistemologically speaking, liberal feminists argue that women have been left out of knowledge-making institutions, and most importantly in the context of reproductive technologies, the institution of medical science. This is simply unfair and has the effect of ignoring or underplaying women's experiences. Making sure women are better represented in important institutions is part of the project of contemporary liberal feminist politics in the pursuit of equality and justice. Even so, liberal feminists tend not to dispute the adequacy of modernist methods of making and collecting knowledge in these institutions (apart from the misogynist mistakes made). Radical and socialist feminists recognise that the liberal feminist insistence on the inclusion of women has paved the way for other feminists to start thinking about *different* knowledges that get produced when subjects different to those traditionally at the centre start producing it. Yet they believe that the epistemological framework of liberal feminism is very limited. They prefer to question deeply and subversively the knowledge we have about reproductive technologies and how women are able to use that knowledge (or not).

For example, is the value of motherhood being reduced by reproductive technologies? Do some reproductive technologies reinforce the construction of the heterosexual nuclear family? Do scientific knowledges about reproductive technologies perpetuate the undervaluing of women's knowledges about themselves, their bodies and their pregnancies? These sorts of questions are very radical indeed as they destabilise traditional and liberal understandings of 'normal' motherhood, 'normal' family structures and 'normal' ways of knowing about sexualities and sexual practices.

By asking these sorts of questions, radical and socialist feminists extend the political reach of liberal feminist politics. Liberal feminists may insist on the political necessity for women to be treated as responsible and mature subjects. But radical and socialist feminist reconsiderations suggest that violence is masquerading as responsibility and that 'normality' is masquerading as maturity. Shifting the meanings of responsibility and normality is a highly political act. Liberal feminists are wary of these sorts of questions because they strongly suggest that private desires and behaviours are social and cultural constructions. Yet all modernist feminists agree that – in their very different ways – feminist political reconsiderations of reproductive technologies improve women's lives.

## Where to now?

This chapter considered modernist feminist theories through the practices of reproductive technologies. It revealed that thinking modernist feminist theory through practice accentuates both the differences between and similarities among modernist feminist theories. In the next chapter I shall think postmodern feminisms through the practices of reproductive technologies on my way to addressing the fundamental question: Is there a gulf between modernist and postmodernist feminisms?

# 4 Postmodernist feminisms and reproductive technologies
## Thinking theory through practice

> We have a developing feminist theory whose intention is to destabilize.
> (Barrett and Phillips, 1992: 1)

What is the postmodern feminist story about reproductive technologies? How do feminist theories influenced by the ideas and values of postmodernism help us to think about the practices and implications of reproductive technologies? How will a discussion of these questions assist in challenging the idea that there is a gulf between modernist and postmodernist feminisms? These are the sorts of questions I opened the last chapter with and clearly they need to be asked in this chapter in order to examine what it means to say there is a gulf between modernist and postmodern feminisms.

As I explained in the preface, I am not claiming that there is only *one* postmodern feminist story (as there isn't *one* modernist feminist story). Nevertheless, there are certain things that distinguish feminisms inspired by modernism compared to those inspired by postmodernism, as the debate about a gulf indicates. And, of course, it is the *significance* of those differences that I am interested in exploring in this book. Clearly each group of feminists believes that the differences are significant otherwise the debate between them would not be so emotive, as I discussed in Chapter 2. It's not that modernist and postmodernist feminists are interested in radically opposed things. After all, from the examples and issues in this book, it is obvious that modernist and postmodernist feminists are all interested, in one way or another, in questions about women's bodies in the context of reproductive technologies. It is more the case that those feminists influenced by postmodernism think and theorise about issues in rather different ways to modernist feminists. The question is, does this matter and, if so, how? In order to address that last question, this chapter will follow a similar format to the last chapter as I shall look at postmodern feminist views on the three categories; the subject, epistemology and politics.

## The subject

> [Postmodern] feminism destabilizes the categories that fellow feminists hold dear.
>
> (Ferguson, 1993: 123)

One of the major categories that postmodern feminists destabilise is the subject. As we saw in the last chapter, modernist feminists considered a number of subjects in the context of reproductive technologies including the woman, the foetus, the father and the doctor/physician/gynaecologist. However, the subject that really matters is always woman, and the crucial thing to do is to recover and/or reassert the centrality and importance of that subject. In contrast, postmodernist feminists reject the idea that there is a recoverable subject or that the primary subject to analyse is woman. Postmodernist feminists are most interested in looking at how subjects get constructed or positioned and at the same time how to destabilise those constructions.

### Constructing subjects

If we recall from Chapters 1 and 2, postmodernist feminists are not interested in making women (or anybody else) into subjects. It's not that they make a *choice* between retaining the subject or not – instead they revisit and destabilise modernist understandings of what the subject is. They argue that there is no essential subject that can be discovered and they vigorously dispute the political effectiveness of the modernist insistence on such a subject upon which identity claims are made. Given this, how might we think about postmodern destabilisations of the subject in the context of the practices and processes of reproductive technologies? As in Chapter 3, I shall introduce several images invoked by the use of reproductive technologies in order to address this question.

### Image 4.1

> *I am 40 years of age and for the past 10 years have been pursuing infertility treatment. This has led to three miscarriages and four unsuccessful IVF treatments. We have spent all our savings and most of our available energy. I am weary of traipsing round infertility*

*clinics, of examinations, injections, operations, treatments. I am weary of failure, and empty years, and feel that it is time to stop and try to somehow accept that we will never have children. However, I don't know what to do next. I always thought that I would be a mother. Now it is not to be. The house is still empty. In the past 10 years I have sat in a dead-end job waiting to become pregnant. Now I feel I have nothing – not even a career to throw myself into. I don't know how to go forward. I don't know how to put a life together, that has meaning and purpose, and happiness, that doesn't include children. Please help me.*

*(Letter to* Private Lives *section of the* Guardian, *5 April 1999: 17)*

*Image 4.2*

*My children cause me the most exquisite suffering of which I have any experience. It is the suffering of ambivalence: the murderous alternation between bitter resentment and raw-edged nerves and blissful gratification and tenderness. Sometimes I seem to myself, in my feelings toward these tiny guiltless beings, a monster of selfishness and intolerance. Their voices wear away at my nerves, their constant needs, above all their need for simplicity and patience, fill me with despair at my own failures, despair too at my fate, which is to serve a function for which I was not fitted. And I am weak sometimes from held in rage. There are times when I feel only death will free us from one another, when I envy the barren woman who has the luxury of her regrets but lives a life of privacy and freedom. And yet at other times I am melted with the sense of their helpless, charming and quite irresistible beauty – their ability to go on loving and trusting – their staunchness and decency and unselfconsciousness. I love them. But it's in the enormity and inevitability of this love that the sufferings lie.*

*(Rich, 1977: 21–22)*

*Image 4.3*

*In 1994 . . . 19 year old Kawana Michelle Ashley . . . shot herself in the stomach . . . she was delivered by an emergency Caesarean section of a baby girl. She [the baby] died April 11. Ashley was charged with third degree murder and manslaughter: newspapers reported allegations that she killed her '6-month-old-fetus' 'by shooting herself in the womb'.*

*(Squier, 1996: 515)*

How do these three images make us think about reproductive technologies? The first two seem to be desperate tales. The first is a very personal and poignant account of a woman undergoing (and 'failing') IVF treatment. What does this tell us about IVF and about the meanings attached to motherhood? The second is another poignant account – not one that obviously involves technology, but nevertheless, one that presents an evocative image of the contradictions and complexities and sufferings of motherhood. The third image appears to relay yet another desperate story. Again this is a story that does not explicitly involve reproductive technologies but it should make us wonder about the different meanings attached to a 'stomach' and a 'womb'. These are three intriguing stories in the context of reproduction. What can we learn from and about them by asking postmodern feminist questions?

### Creating subjects – mothers

What makes a mother? How do we understand what it means to be a mother? What are the various meanings given to motherhood? These are some of the questions a postmodern feminist might ask. Of course, we may want to claim that a mother is simply a woman who has or cares for a child. But this does not tell us very much about how we think about what it means to be a good or a bad mother, for example. It doesn't tell us much about the processes of becoming a mother (as in learning what a mother is, as opposed to giving birth). Modernist feminists may ask similar questions, as they are also interested in theorising about the values attached to being a mother. As a way to illustrate this they might, for example, draw our attention to how differently we think about 'mothering' and 'fathering'. These feminists (especially liberal feminists) have also traditionally been interested in ameliorating the negative effects that giving birth to and caring for children have had on women, such as preventing women from enjoying the full benefits of (well) paid employment. And clearly radical feminists have been particularly keen on revaluing the role and practices of mothering. Generally speaking, many modernist feminists are concerned about the role that reproductive technologies are playing in taking the power of giving birth away from women – as I discussed in Chapter 3.

But modernist feminists approach these kinds of questions with a particular set of assumptions and beliefs in place. Radical and socialist feminists share a belief in the constraining and constructing nature of the structures of patriarchy and capitalism. These structures have the effect of dictating (to a lesser or greater extent) the process and practices of becoming mothers. Liberal feminists do not share this structural view but they do share with radical and socialist feminists ideas about the subject (mother) who is impacted upon (for good or bad). As we know, postmodern feminisms do not share this view of the subject which begs the crucial question 'What effect does discarding the foundationalist and essentialist baggage attached to the subject make?

In order to address this question, let us look at the first two images. In one sense the stories are similar. They both exude an air of desperation – one desperate at having 'failed' IVF treatment with the result that this woman fears she will face a future without children; in the second a woman expresses the suffering she feels as she tries to cope with the demands and contradictory experiences of being a mother of small children. But the stories are also different in that one tells a story of infertility and the other a story of fertility. Bearing in mind that postmodern feminists are not looking for a 'true' story – what story can be told about what a 'mother is' (or is not) by reading these two tales?

## Resisting/reconstructing subjects

Despite the sadness the women telling these stories express – these tales can be read as examples of subjects resisting and deconstructing dominant stories about what it means to be a mother and/or a fulfilled person. The 40 year old woman in the Image 4.1 asking for help about how to enjoy life and go forward without children might be described as being in 'a moment' of resistance and deconstruction. The postmodern feminist task is not to discover what was going on in her mind when she wrote the letter, nor is it to provide an agenda for institutional or personal change. It is rather to ask questions about how ways of thinking about motherhood, technology and purpose in life have been constructed and reinforced.

One avenue that this process of thinking and deconstruction can lead to would include, for example, a 'deconstruction of the desperateness' that underpins this letter. It does appear to be the case that this woman is desperate because of infertility. Clearly there are very strong motivations for her to have spent ten years pursuing the birth of a baby via IVF. The costs – emotional, physical and financial – are obviously great. Rather than locate the source of this desperation in the realms of 'natural maternal drives' or the constitutive nature of patriarchy and/or capitalism (or anything else foundationally based), postmodern feminists trace the ways the interweaving stories about fertility and infertility and ideas about motherhood and fulfilled lives have developed. For example, since the birth of the first 'test-tube baby' in 1978, stories about conceptions achieved by late twentieth-century reproductive technologies have proliferated, especially in the popular press and in popular guides for the public (Franklin, 1997: 89). By (re)reading these stories, feminists, using some of the techniques of postmodernism such as deconstruction, can tell alternative stories.

We can return to Image 3.1 to think further about this.

> *For the Hortons and an estimated one million other couples in Britain striving to overcome childlessness, doctors can now resort to a remarkable and increasing number of treatments. Advances in the use of drugs, surgical techniques and in vitro fertilisation mean that babies are now being born to couples who until quite recently would have been described as hopeless cases.*
>
> *(Prentice,* The Sunday Times, *1986: 10,*
> *quoted in Franklin, 1997: 89–90)*

If when reading this we already hold the belief that having one's own child is a natural or instinctive drive, then this necessarily limits the kinds of questions we can ask or ideas we can pursue. It would seem logical to embrace the use of science to 'overcome childlessness'. However, if all such foundational beliefs in the realm of nature or instinct are abandoned, the possibility arises for other sorts of questioning. For example, we might ask: 'How did having one's own child come to matter so much?' Asking this question may then make us think further about the issue of childlessness, which can lead to all manner of intriguing insights.

For example, the issue of childlessness seems to be integrally tied up with ideas about social belonging and identity, which is often presented as having social and genetic elements. As *The Warnock Report*[1] claims,

> [C]hildlessness can be a source of stress even to those who have deliberately chosen it . . . They may feel excluded from a whole range of human activity . . . in addition to social pressures to have children there is, for many, a powerful urge to perpetuate their genes through a new generation. This desire cannot be assuaged by adoption.
>
> (Warnock, 1985: 9, quoted in Franklin, 1997: 90–91)

It would appear that the idea that it is normal and right for couples to have their own children has historically drawn upon entrenched social practices and strong beliefs about powerful genetic drives to reproduce. Over time this has done a great deal of work in establishing what the 'social and natural facts of infertility' are (ibid.: 91).

### What does opening up of questions about the construction of the subject do?

> Although the subject . . . is socially constructed in discursive practices, she none the less exists as a thinking, feeling subject and social agent, capable of resistance and innovations produced out of the clash between contradictory subject positions and practices. She is also a subject able to reflect upon the discursive relations which constitute her and the society in which she lives, and able to choose from the options available.
>
> (Weedon, 1987: 125)

One form of 'discursive practice' or set of 'discursive relations' that has clearly had a strong impact is in the realm of having one's own children, especially in the context of contemporary heterosexual marriage. However, the experiences of motherhood are often at odds with the joys that having one's own children is supposed to bring – as the story told in Image 4.2 sharply demonstrates. It might be the case that feminist postmodern deconstructions and decentring of the subject could open up a space for a woman to think about the inadequacies felt by either being a new mother or not being a mother at all. For example, a new mother is often catapulted into a discourse of motherhood in which she is exposed to child care demands framed by contemporary social relations. This may leave the woman with feelings of being an unnatural or a bad parent. The expectation that she will meet all the child's needs, often single-handedly, and achieve personal fulfilment from this, may lead to her feeling depressed and unable to cope. In the contemporary west, the demands or expectation that women have a fulfilling paid career as well as being a good mother can lead to all sorts of frustrations (Weedon, 1987: 33–34). Being aware of these competing subject positions might offer the frustrated mother (a subject able to reflect) a new subject position from which to make sense of her situation, a position which makes her the subject rather than the cause of the contradictions which she is living, 'as the subject of a range of conflicting discourses, she is *subjected* to their contradictions at great emotional cost' (ibid.). As subjects reflecting upon the 'discursive relations which constitute [them]', and quite clearly resulting in 'great emotional cost', the women in Images 4.1 and 4.2 may find a way to reconstitute themselves as different subjects via their practices of questioning and resisting.

In each of these images both women appear to be questioning their capabilties and lamenting their failures. Indeed, each uses the word 'failure' – and each locates that failure largely within herself. But in the process of lamenting it, they are both questioning – implicitly if not explicitly – the construction of themselves as someone who 'should be a mother' or as someone who is 'failing at being a (good) mother'. Each of these women may not articulate what they are doing as 'deconstructing and resisting the construction of the subject of mother' – mostly they simply feel bad and are searching for help. But when we read their stories as postmodern feminists, we can set in train a plethora of questions which will open up all sorts of ways through which we can think about the construction of the subject – in this example the subject of mother.

### Further deconstructions

Working without the foundationalist and essentialist commitments characteristic of modernist feminisms, postmodern feminists are led down avenues of 'endless questioning' which modernist feminists are unable or are unprepared to go down. If the intent is neither to 'prove patriarchy and/or capitalism', nor to 'prove women's equality', then there is less incentive to stop deconstructing, as arriving at an 'end point' is *not* the point. This, together with a commitment to deconstruct *everything*, arguably enables postmodern feminists to interrogate subjectivities and territories that appear to move away from women/gender.

For example, in the context of limitless deconstruction, feminist theorising itself will not be exempt. Therefore one might ask: Why are feminists so interested in asking questions about the subjectivities of mothers and the impact of reproductive technologies on mothers? What effects does this have? What is the effect, for example, of the conflation or easy association of woman/mother in much modernist feminist analysis? One answer might be that this conflation carries with it 'a necessary horizon of heterosexuality' (Flax, 1993: 67). In societies saturated with heterosexist assumptions and values, we don't usually question how a mother got pregnant, which permits an almost automatic assumption of the existence somewhere of a man/husband/father.

In our current discourses, woman/mother often presumes or requires the simultaneous existence of two related dyads: child/

mother, father/mother. Consider, for example, the curious term 'single' mother. How can a mother be single, since by definition she is a being in some relation to an Other? Obviously she is 'single' because she 'lacks' a husband; she operates outside the normal rules of the Name of the Father. Maternity without paternity is a deviant form.

(Ibid.: 67)

Think back to Images 4.1 and 4.2. Who is the 'we' that the first woman mentions (only) once? Did any of us make heterosexist assumptions on first reading this image? And where is the 'we' in the second image? Neither of these women *may* be explicitly questioning the heterosexist logic that underpins their construction as mothers – but when reading these stories as postmodern feminists, it is a questioning that becomes necessary.

### Legitimate subjects?

As many of you may know, the writer of the second image – Adrienne Rich – went on to write one of the most influential early articles on 'compulsory heterosexuality' (Rich, 1986). In this she claimed that heterosexuality is a political institution and we are all – straight, gay or anything else – deeply affected by it. More that two decades on, it can be argued that the practices and processes of reproductive technologies play a part in the reproduction of the 'legitimate sexual and reproducing subject' – especially through the subject of 'mother'. In the provision of IVF for example, it is difficult for women other than those in conventional heterosexual marriages to have access to IVF. This discriminatory practice appears to be sharply at odds with the (presumed) genetic/biological drive that women are traditionally deemed to have which, as we have seen, feeds into and reinforces many contemporary stories about fertility and infertility.

A popular guide on infertility treatment waxes lyrical on this topic.

Call it a cosmic spark or spiritual fulfilment, biological need or human destiny – the desire for a family rises unbidden from our genetic souls. In centuries past, to multiply was to prevail – the family was stronger and better able to survive, than the individual.

(Franklin, 1997: 207)

Taking the idea of biological destiny to its logical conclusion, one would be led to the conclusion that *all* women shared it. Yet it is

very interesting to note that many in the medical profession think it is
unethical or immoral to allow lesbian women to reproduce via IVF.
Patrick Steptoe (half of the medical partnership responsible for the
birth of the first test-tube baby in 1978),

> simultaneously believed that all women have a biological drive to
> reproduce, and that it is immoral for lesbians or single women to
> have children. Thus, for socially acceptable women, biology
> should be destiny, whereas for socially unacceptable women, the
> demands of biology should be restricted by social sanctions.
>
> (Ibid.: 208)

Questions that might emerge from this discussion include, 'Who is fit to
reproduce or be reproduced?' Many conventionally sanctioned stories
depict lesbian women as not 'fit' to reproduce – and paradoxically
'virgin' lesbian women are deemed to be even *less* fit to reproduce.
When the popular press 'revealed' that 'virgin' lesbian women were
being allowed to have IVF treatment in some clinics, a furore erupted.
It was bad enough that such women wanted to have babies, but without
ever having experienced male penile penetration, this, in the popular
imagination, was even more appalling (Shildrick, 1997: 188). Perhaps
reproductive technologies are in part, 'technologies of heterosexuality'
(Steinberg, 1997: 69).

To be a 'legitimate reproducing subject', a mother may have to
conform to certain sexual subject positions (which doesn't preclude
resisting those subject positions), but what about the 'reproduced'?
Who is fit to be reproduced? Let us revisit Image 3.2 to think further
about this.

> *The [prenatal screening] tests permit parents who know they are at
> risk of bearing a defective baby to conceive, assured that if the test is
> positive, they can abort and try again for a healthy baby ... [I]t is
> heartless to deny parents access to medical technology that permits
> them to avoid giving birth to an incurably ill or severely retarded
> infant.*
>
> *(Rushing and Onorato, 1989: 273)*

This is a profound set of statements. Think of the words used – a 'defective baby', a 'healthy baby', a 'retarded baby'. For some parents it
might seem heartless to deny them this test. For others it might be
read as a terrible indictment of contemporary values – a 'throw-away
baby society'. Isn't this what women used to do in centuries gone by

because of poverty and starvation – literally throw their babies away because they could not care for them? Of course this still happens today – but does it matter what the reason for being unable 'to care' is? Is 'discarding' a baby because of abnormality 'better' than discarding it because of poverty?

Some of the responses to the publication of a Royal College of Physicians report on *Prenatal Diagnosis* (1989) illustrate the intellectual and emotional turmoil that the issue of aborting 'defective foetuses' raises. The report claimed that, 'unless prenatal diagnosis is to be devoid of practical application when it reveals a major defect in the foetus, a responsible doctor must discuss with the parents the option of terminating that pregnancy' (1989: 49). Clearly the phrase 'practical application' here means abortion. Following the publication of this report, a short piece appeared in the *Guardian* newspaper which reinforced some of the claims of the report by saying that gaps in prenatal testing left 2,000 children each year with incurable diseases. This was the case because 'health authorities have failed to offer couples the most advanced prenatal screening tests'.

A flurry of letters appeared in the *Guardian* following this short report. Many were from parents of children with Down's Syndrome arguing that their children's lives were worth saving and valuable (Orme; Brennan, letters to the *Guardian*, 15 September 1989). Others raised the spectre of Adolf Hitler:

> Britain went to war 50 years ago on behalf of Hitler's victims – and he was rightly vilified for his medical experiments on women and children and his Final Solution, i.e. death for all those considered inferior. Now, in the Report on Prenatal Diagnosis and Genetic Screening, our Royal College of Physicians proposes the same solution for unborn handicapped babies – kill them by abortion.
> (Waddelove, letter to the *Guardian*, 15 September 1989)

Further letters appeared decrying the eugenic base of prenatal diagnosis intimated by the report. One correspondent stated 'what the members of the working party who produced the report on Prenatal Diagnosis and Genetic Counselling are really saying is: We cannot cure, so instead we kill' (Henry, letter to the *Guardian*, 19 September 1989). Another pointed to the fact that prenatal diagnosis often cannot predict the severity of the disability accurately (Hughes, letter to the *Guardian*, 19 September 1989). This echoes Martin Orme's earlier letter saying that his 15 year old son who has Down's Syndrome would like to ask whether it would not be fairer to wait until the child is born before deciding whether the handicap is bad enough to warrant killing (Orme, letter to the *Guardian*, 15 September 1989)? A physician's reply on 19 September argued that what stops us moving from aborting handicapped foetuses to killing handicapped infants is 'common sense and humanity' (Goodman, letter to the *Guardian*, 19 September 1989).

What is a postmodern feminist to make of this? The ethical and moral dilemmas concerning a 'woman's right to choose' and 'the right to life' are very complex here. One reason for the extra complexity is that these babies are usually (initially) wanted babies. This is not a question of a woman not wanting to have a baby, it's about not wanting a *particular* baby; a 'defective' one. So perhaps we might ask the question again – who is deemed fit to be reproduced? Or more appropriately for a postmodern feminist, how are such concepts as 'normality', 'healthy', 'retarded' and 'defective' produced and then attached to subjects?

This question can lead to a whole swathe of interrogations about how 'deviant humans' become constituted. Who were those deemed not fit to reproduce, or be reproduced (or even exist) in Nazi Germany? Homosexuals, mental defectives and Jews? If we recall the physician's comment above that what stops us moving from aborting handi-capped foetuses to killing handicapped infants is 'common sense and humanity', a postmodern feminist might ask: How do ideas and stories about common sense and humanity construct normal and abnormal and indeed the distinction between foetuses and babies? On that latter distinction let me briefly refer to Image 4.3 – did Kawana Ashley shoot her baby or was she trying to abort her foetus or did she attempt suicide?

How do we know the answers to any of these questions? The physi-cian I refer to above appears to think the answer is easy. Modernist humanists who believe in a fundamental right to life on the basis of being human might also think the answer is easy using foundational beliefs about humanity. But as we know, postmodern feminists dis-card beliefs in foundational bases for knowledge. How then do they think about the production of knowledge in the arena of reproductive technologies?

## Epistemology

### *How does knowledge create subjectivities?*

Postmodernists are not interested in discovering 'the truth' but are concerned to analyse how knowledge and truth are produced (Scott,

1993: 438). In addition to this, postmodernists generally think it is important to illustrate the assumptions and inadequacies of the epistemological foundations and techniques of modernism (Yeatman, 1994: 28). This all implies that postmodern feminists are not looking for true knowledge about reproductive technologies or the 'answers' to the questions I raised above. Instead they are looking at how reproductive technologies create or constitute knowledges and subjectivities as well as interrogating how answers to questions about reproductive technologies are arrived at and what effects those answers have.

When postmodernists think, speak or write about knowledge, they clearly do not mean simply facts or information. If modernists think of knowledge as something that explains events and things in general and enables the creation of new things (such as technologies, weapons, medicines), postmodernists interrogate the way knowledge and its effects (material and ideological) construct how we feel, think, know and understand. What we 'know' and how knowledge is practised in the everyday creates further knowledges. We 'know' things because we 'do' or 'practise' them. In other words, we get to know things – and crucially we become and know ourselves (subjectivities) – through these daily practices. Given all this, how might we think about reproductive technologies as postmodern feminists?

### *Disciplinary practices – 'disciplined subjects'*

To interrogate how daily practices create these knowledges and subjectivities, many postmodern feminists draw on the work of Michel Foucault, especially his work on 'disciplinary practices' (1977). They use it to interrogate how certain practices can render the body into a regulated set of subjectivities – a kind of 'docile body'. These sorts of practices are effected and made effective,

> not through the threat of violence or force, but rather by creating desires, attaching individuals to specific identities, and establishing norms which individuals and their behaviours and bodies are judged and against which they police themselves.
>
> (Sawicki, 1991: 68)

This way of thinking about how a body is regulated and disciplined illustrates one of the differences between modernist and postmodernist thinking. The effect of 'creating desires', 'attaching individuals to specific identities' and 'establishing norms', is not tied to any structural driving force such as patriarchy or capitalism as a way to explain any of these things. Rather it is a way of tracing and illustrating how bodies can be regulated, monitored and disciplined, which impacts on how we understand and 'know' specific bodies – whether they are our own or others. How does this work in the context of IVF or prenatal screening for example?

The sophisticated techniques of observation, monitoring and surveillance that such reproductive technologies involve have made women's bodies and foetuses much more visible in ways that have arguably facilitated the creation of them as 'new objects and subjects of medical as well as legal and state intervention' (ibid.: 83–84). Examples of subjects created by the new technologies include: infertile women; surrogate and genetically impaired mothers; mothers whose bodies are not fit for pregnancy (either biologically or socially); mothers who are psychologically unfit for fertility treatments; mothers whose wombs are hostile environments to foetuses; mothers who are deemed 'negligent' for not choosing to undergo tests, abort genetically 'deficient' foetuses, or consent to Caesarean sections.

A whole host of new subjects have thereby been created by these surveillance techniques and the knowledges they produce, and these new subjects are created in ways that they become *self-disciplining*. Think of the women in Images 4.1 and 4.2. The '40 year old infertile woman' and the 'suffering fertile woman'. Each of these women 'knows herself' through dominant ideas about what it means to be a 'good mother' and/or 'fulfilled person'. And they have disciplined themselves accordingly. Here, it is important to be clear that the word 'discipline' does not imply self-punishment (although each of these women is clearly suffering). It is more the case that these women come to 'know' themselves and therefore 'be' themselves through dominant ideas and that they feel and act accordingly. Thus, the process of 'being watched' or constituted elicits a process of 'watching and constituting yourself'. Let us think about this a little more through the example of ultrasound.

### Ultrasound – a benign invasion?

The practice of having one or more ultrasound scans (alternatively called sonograms) during pregnancy has become a regular occurrence in the western world (Mitchell and Georges, 1998: 105). Having a 'window on the womb' is commonly understood to be one of those 'miracles of modern science'. It is a popular technology and is presented and mostly understood to be one of the least invasive forms of reproductive technologies – indeed women/couples expect it as a way to receive their first 'baby picture'. But is it such a 'non-invasive' event? In medical and popular terms, the word 'invasive' is taken to mean a cut or entry through the skin in some form or other; by a needle or a scalpel, for example. The body is thereby conceptualised to end at the skin, and what counts as invasive is an entry through the skin; the invasion is the crossing of the fleshly border. Ultrasound scanning is therefore deemed to be non-invasive as no cut is made.

But surely there is an invasion of sorts; even if this is just sound-waves. Perhaps the sense of invasion is best understood in the context of some of the possible *effects* of the visualisation. For many modernist feminists the increasing subjectification of the foetus, objectification of the mother and the characterisation of the mother/foetus relationship as antagonistic leads to all manner of unpleasant outcomes. Post-modern feminists' main concern, however, is not to prove that such technologies or the effects of them are either good or bad – but instead to investigate how subjectivities and knowledges are constructed by the practice of them.

In order to make more sense of this let us take a closer look at Image 4.3.

*Image 4.3*

> *In 1994 . . . 19 year old Kawana Michelle Ashley . . . shot herself in the stomach . . . [s]he was delivered by an emergency Caesarean section of a baby girl. She [the baby] died April 11. Ashley was charged with third degree murder and manslaughter: newspapers reported allegations that she killed her '6-month-old-fetus' 'by shoot-ing herself in the womb'.*
>
> *(Squier, 1996: 515)*

This is a very tragic tale. But what went on here? A death of a baby at the hands of her mother? A 'successful' abortion? An attempted suicide? It's likely that a modernist feminist would want to get to 'the truth' behind the story. Most of us want to get to 'the truth' a lot of the time – and this desire or hope certainly underpins the idea behind newspaper reporting (if rare in practice!) and the judicial process. But what might a postmodernist feminist ask in the context of how repro-ductive technologies create subjectivities and knowledges?

We don't know whether Kawana Ashley had undergone any medical treatment or technological intervention during her pregnancy. It seems unlikely if we believe newspaper reports that, 'she didn't have enough money for an abortion' (ibid.). But in the context of our interrogation of the construction of subjectivities, it does not matter whether this particular woman had the use of any reproductive technologies. The point is that the use of these technologies in the wider community produces new knowledges about foetuses, mothers and babies which can impact on the subjectivities of all of us.

Ultrasound technology has impacted on our imaginations in quite profound ways. The imaging of the foetus has become increasingly popular over the last twenty-five years and one effect has been to solidify the recognition of the foetus as a separate entity – often in need of protection. This construction has clearly been used by the anti-abortion movement from the production of the film *A Silent Scream*[2] to the bombarding of British members of parliament with plastic dolls meant to resemble 18 week old foetuses whilst they were debating a change to the Abortion Act. The main idea behind both of these is to create in people's imaginations the idea or knowledge that the foetus is a fully human and separate being. The postmodern point is not to argue that this either is or is not the case, the point is to interrogate its effects, though this does not stop postmodernists arguing that some of the effects are disturbing: 'The case of Kawana Ashley embodies tendencies nurtured in the practices of reproductive technologies – tendencies with profoundly disturbing implications for us as individuals and as social beings' (Squier, 1996: 516).

The ubiquitous use of ultrasound and its visual currency in the late twentieth century has arguably played a large part in positing the foetus as a subject; downplaying the gestating woman's role, and enhancing the tendency to conceive of the foetus and the mother as social, medical and legal antagonists (ibid.). How this has worked out in the daily life of Kawana Ashley is that her attempted suicide is rendered invisible. She is reported to have shot herself in the *womb* and not *stomach*. In other words, the new knowledge created via ultrasound has created a new subject – the foetus. One effect of this in rights-based cultures is to encourage hierarchies of subjects to whom hierarchical rights are then attached.

### Foetus in control?

Manifestly her body is already colonized by a fetus with greater definitional rights than she herself has.

(Squier, 1996: 531)

This idea that a mother's body – Kawana Ashley's – has become colonised by a foetus might seem bizarre. But even medical textbooks invoke this kind of imagery with, for example, descriptions of the foetus as a 'little commander in the womb' (Martin, 1998: 134). Let us think about this notion of foetus as coloniser/commander by introducing a fourth image.

*Image 4.4*

> *Allow me to tell you, dear human brethren, that I am the fruit of a unique mutation. Even in my original cell phase, I knew exactly where I was going. Can one even maintain that I was 'conceived' in the true sense of the term? I doubt it. Had I not always existed? . . . I am living proof that the fetus is not man's initial state, but his total state, after which it is all downhill . . . I am my dearest enigma to myself: I never tire of trying to solve myself. Why, I can affirm that I've come a long way, I'm fine today – to quote dear old Hegel, 'Knowledge as the self-conceiving self' – if you catch my drift. My peculiarity? I am only a brain, a giant intellectual apparatus.*
> *( Bruckner, 1994: 79, quoted in Squier, 1996: 526)*

This extract is from the novel *The Divine Child* by Pascal Bruckner (1994). In the novel a woman – Madeleine Barthelemey – is pregnant. Prior to the confirmation that she is carrying twins (via an ultrasound scan) she had signed on for a rigorous course of prenatal education – meaning education for the *foetus*, not the mother. This means that a barrage of information is fed into her womb through a range of miniature speakers inserted in every available maternal orifice. This appears to be effective as one morning she hears, 'two voices twanging and begging: "More, more"!' (Squier, 1996: 521). Following the scan she names the twins Louis and Celene. Celene is born, but to the horror of those watching, she has appeared to have 'lost' all her prenatal education and emerges as a squealing, mucus-covered infant. Louis, having seen what birth has done to his sister, refuses to be born, relying on the same visualisation technology that earlier was used to monitor him in the uterus.

> His garret of mucus now resembled the instrument panel in a jet cockpit: several monitors, a video screen, earphones, dozens of flashing signal lights, a computer terminal, an ultrasophisticated radiophone, and a fax machine situated him at the center of a gigantic communications network, an immense nervous system that linked him to the four corners of the world.
> (Ibid.: 522)

Louis' 'life' carries on like this for five years in which time he becomes a fascination for the world's scientists and physicians. A group of Japanese scientists offer him a holographic device that can project moving images on to the lining of the womb and Louis becomes convinced that he is almost 'divine' – invincible perhaps, as his view of himself in Image 4.4 tells us. But the whole process of 'willed regression' (refusing to go forward and be born) begins to come up against its own limits and Louis finds himself fossilising and returning to his embryonic state. Threatening to take the world with him in apocalyptic fashion, Madeleine and her obstetrician scheme to have Louis delivered and destroyed by high-frequency ultrasound waves. They are ultimately successful.

In this bizarre tale one can clearly argue that there has been a 'major shift in the site of privileged subjectivity' (ibid.: 523). The woman's body has indeed been taken over by the foetus and the author of the novel provides us with 'an embryonic or foetal subject whose rights exceed those of the already born' (ibid.). The story is clearly an imagined 'science fiction' type scenario. How, you might be wondering, does it help us think about postmodern feminist thinking about epistemology? And how, in turn, does this help us to think about reproductive technologies in the everyday? In order to address those questions I want to move on to postmodern feminist ideas about politics.

## Politics

### *What's a constructed subjectivity to 'do'?*

For postmodern feminists, subjectivities, epistemologies and politics are all deeply intertwined. Although most modernist feminists accept that the three impact upon each other, they tend to think of them as affecting each other in a progressive, linear fashion. What this means is that modernists usually think of the subject as pre-existing, then epistemological practices impact on this subject, and politics is a necessary activity to achieve specific emancipatory or liberatory ends (if the subject is deemed to be repressed). Postmodern feminists do not think it works like this. Think of the phrase I have used frequently throughout this book – 'In the face of what is, what shall we do?' – as a way to get into discussions about the connections between feminist theory and political practice. Postmodern feminists would probably alter this question to read something like, 'In the face of what we *do*, what becomes?' Or to put it another way, what are the effects of practices?

Because postmodernists believe that things (concepts, actions, subjects) do not have any essential meanings – they are given meaning – this implies that a great deal of power is to be found in the way stories are told about things, or the way in which they are presented. Telling stories – different stories – can therefore be a powerful political practice in and of itself. Think of the story told in Image 4.3 about Kawana Ashley. Clearly a judicial reading of this story is that this woman – this subject – is a suspected murderer because of her use of a loaded gun targeted at the/her foetus. The postmodern argument is that the visualisation technology of ultrasound has helped to construct the foetus as a subject with rights and in an antagonistic relationship with its mother and her rights. Imagining the foetus as a thing without rights – perhaps until it is born – would give rise to a different story; one that constructed the woman as attempting to take her own life. If a man shot himself in the stomach, it would be difficult to think of this act as being anything else than one of self-harm and/or a suicide attempt.

Retelling the story in a way that illustrates how subjects can be constructed differently tells us something about the power of story-telling – and stories provide us with knowledge. To make this point, stories can be told about anything – they do not have to be explicitly linked to 'reality'. Telling the story of Louis can serve as an imaginative device to open up thinking about how subjects get constructed. This also provides a way to trace how knowledge-making institutions and practices construct meanings and therefore subjectivities and knowledges. Thus the postmodern political activity here is more to do with illustrating how subjects 'get said' rather than thinking about what subjects do or providing subjects with an idea about what to do. Thinking about Kawana Ashley in this context – is 'she said' as a murderer'? Is 'she said' as an abortionist? Is 'she said' as an attempted suicide? That the judicial establishment can even start to imagine her as a potential murderer only 'becomes' because of new stories about the mother and foetus nurtured by reproductive technologies such as ultrasound.

Other traditional and authoritative establishments such as medical and biological science have also played a part in these constructions. The duality of 'the pregnant body' has always been something of a enigma for medical practitioners. As we know from decades of feminist research on the production of medical and biological knowledge, the standard, in terms of both intellectual models and the human form, has been that of the 'male/masculine'. Women – and especially pregnant women – have always been constructed as deviating from the standard. That a pregnant woman's body does not expel the foetus as a 'foreign body' has always been something of a mystery to medical practitioners. But the interconnectedness between mother and foetus has been subject to disconnection because of the practices of reproductive technologies giving rise to a story about Kawana Ashley that separates her and her/the foetus in crucially important ways – making her a suspected murderer.

## A docile and desperate politics?

But this can all sound like a politics of despair. Does it imply that subjects such as Kawana Ashley can only be read as docile and disciplined bodies impacted on by authorities in abusive ways?

Let me introduce a fifth image to think further about my last question.

## Image 4.5

> *[Zelda is] forced into a cybernetic alliance with the professor's machinery . . . the machinery of induction threatens Zelda's ability to renegotiate subjectivity through labor and birth; the machine/ physician has entered her by way of needles and monitors, recreating her in his image. But, like Frankenstein's monster, Zelda offends her creators. She screams and shits on them in a semiotic fury.*
> *(Baines 1983, quoted in Adams, 1994: 57)*

This is another science fiction story – *The Birth Machine* written by Elizabeth Baines in 1983. In the story Zelda's labour is induced as part of a clinical trial of convenience inductions. Her doctor is an eminent professor and her husband's superior. As such, her husband – Roland – is reluctant to question the doctor's decision to induce and regulate Zelda's labour a week before her due date. Zelda is puzzled about the reason for the induction but when she asks about it, she cannot understand the answer she is given and tells her husband: 'That's just it, Roland, they didn't say. They said there's nothing *wrong*.'

The conversation between her and her husband about the induced labour leaves her feeling confused and frustrated. One reading of this suggests that,

> the words hung between them like a puzzle, a jumbled chain, upside down. Inconsistent, not making sense. She saw herself through Roland's eyes: lay person, out of touch, to whom the words of the [medical] priesthood couldn't have any meaning, would only come as an arcane jumble; pregnant woman, blown

with hormones that made her flush and cry and jump in fright – a caricature of femininity, too emotionally turbulent to interpret plain English when it hits against her eardrum.

(Ibid.: 54)

The description of Zelda's experiences seems horrific. Here we can surely see a woman abused by the practices of medicine and science? And a woman forced into an induction of labour for convenience and then not being understood, or more accurately not being *heard*, when she tries to work out what is going on and why she feels so bad? Surely this is a woman in pain? A woman who has been almost totally objectified by scientific needs as well as her husband. It's not that the foetus has become the primary subject – both foetus and mother seem subordinated to the needs of the husband and the scientific/medical establishment.

But to represent Zelda as a victim of patriarchal practices would simply replicate modernist ideas about subjectivity – a subject impacted upon and repressed by the powerful. As postmodern feminists, we can re-present and re-imagine Zelda as always in the process of constitution and therefore can resist and renegotiate the construction of her subjectivity. The postmodern idea being to rewrite the story of repression rather than as a way to liberate the subject herself. Although the 'machinery of induction threatens Zelda's ability to renegotiate subjectivity through labor and birth', she resists their need for her to 'behave' and 'screams and shits on them in a semiotic fury'. Going against hospital expectations that labouring women should refrain from indulging in 'degrading scenes', Zelda 'raves and her body contorts . . . Her disorder is infectious. The entire system, hospital and staff, are potentially vulnerable to the same disease that afflicts the maddened woman in labor' (ibid.: 58).

An emergency Caesarean section is performed and a drugged Zelda 'floats away from the scene and, from this alienated vantage point, watches them remove her son from her body' (ibid.). When the drugs wear off, Zelda 'steals' her medical chart and finds that she has been betrayed – an induction was not necessary. Her prior inarticulateness and emotional turbulence can now be revisited in ways that make sense to Zelda. She is no longer in their control, She steals a nurse's cloak, 'steals' her son and leaves the hospital. One way that this story has been told represents Zelda as a 'caricature of femininity' (ibid.: 54). But Zelda having 'stirred and disturbed their order' gives herself new names – ones that potentially make her the authority on her condition and behaviour.

### A politics of disturbance and resistance

> Within a postmodern politics, there are no guaranteed outcomes,
> no train of victory narratives to hop on for the ride to glory.
> Instead, there is a range of strategic responses to subjections
> including the multiplication of resistances, the scrambling of
> master-codes, and the nurturing of new and hybrid forms.
>
> (Farquhar, 1996: 185–186)

The comment in the above quote that postmodern politics is not about
a 'victory narrative to hop on for the ride to glory' can be read as
targeting modernist politics with the latter's general aim of distinguish-
ing truth from power with the idea of ending up with successful liberatory or emancipatory outcomes. This is not the goal for feminist
postmodernists. Instead they illustrate and interrogate how subjects
'get said' through a 'multiplication of resistances', which implies that
a whole range of things can be used as political sites – including deconstructing how stories get told. Remember that stories here means how
anything is given meaning: 'Contests for the meanings of writing are a
major form of contemporary political struggle. Releasing the play of
writing is deadly serious' (Haraway, 1991: 175). And of course 'writing'
does not imply only the written word. Stories are 'written' and told in
all manner of ways including: vocally, visually (think of ultrasound),
sign language, aurally, via metaphor, via imaginations and so on.
A feminist postmodern politics of disturbance and resistance is intent
upon disturbing these meanings – or in general disturbing the 'order
of things' – quite simply 'messing things up': 'Try to go back through
the names they've given you . . . When you stir, you disturb their
order. You upset everything. You break the circle of their habits . . .
their knowledge, their desire' (Irigaray, 1985: 205, 207).

If we think of the example of Zelda from Image 4.5 – she clearly
'disturbed the order' of the hospital and upset everything. But it is
important to remember that the postmodern political concern is not
about liberating the subject – Zelda in this example. Taking the idea
of 'scrambling master-codes' referred to in the opening quote of this
section, this necessarily implies scrambling the 'master-codes' or
dominant codes or systems of meaning and understanding of traditional feminist theorising. So the subject of woman as she has been
constructed by feminist theories or anything else must be destabilised
also.

## What is the postmodernist feminist 'story' about reproductive technologies?

As I have made clear, there is not one story – whether modernist or postmodernist – about anything. In this chapter I have focused mainly on one aspect of postmodern practice, namely the interrogation and destabilisation of subjects and knowledge-making practices. My main intention has been to provide an idea of the main differences between postmodern and modernist feminist ways of thinking about reproductive technologies especially in the context of feminist politics. Retelling the stories presented in the images evoked by some of the uses of reproductive technologies and suggesting how we might trace some of the ideas and beliefs which inform these images is in itself an example of feminist postmodern political practice. One of the main aims of this book is to explore and challenge the idea that there is a gulf between modernist and postmodern feminisms, particularly in the realm of feminist politics, which is what I shall now move on to in Chapter 5.

## Notes

1 The Warnock Committee was formed in the United Kingdom in 1982 to advise the government, parliament and the general public on matters of human fertility and embryology. It was headed by the philosopher Dame Mary Warnock.
2 This film was made by Dr Bernard Natahanson in his capacity as member of the US-based National Right to Life Committee and purported to show a real-time ultrasound imaging of a 12-week old foetus being aborted. With organ music playing in the background, the narrator leads us through the procedure with the intention of showing the pain (the 'silent scream') that the foetus experiences (see Rosalind Pollack Petchesky, 'Foetal Images: the Power of Visual Culture in the Politics of Reproduction' in Michelle Stanworth, 1987, pp. 57–80).

# 5 'Recovering' feminisms?

Is there a significant gulf between 1970s modernist feminisms and 1990s postmodernist feminisms? Let me start by summarising the argument for the case that there is a theoretical gulf between these two bodies of feminism.

## Theoretical gulf

Modernist feminists generally think about the subject of woman in different ways to postmodernist feminists. Earlier, I introduced the image of an apple and an onion to help understand that difference – the (modernist) apple having an ultimate core whereas the (postmodern) onion is layered over nothing. In the realm of epistemology, modernist feminists tend to adhere to a belief in the ultimate existence of true and untainted knowledge. Of course in practice there is not much of this 'innocent' knowledge around – but the modernist feminist aim is to strive towards achieving it. This is a vital political practice for modernist feminists as it promises the separation of truth from sexist and misogynist power and prejudice. The idea or belief that the 'truth will out' still has a profound impact on the modernist mind-set.

Following on from the modernist aim of discovering and demon-strating the truth, the point of feminist theory is to *do* something about the sexist and misogynist injustices and untruths that are uncovered. In the context of modernist feminisms, this has led to a variety of demands such as for the right to vote, the right to be free from violence, to have equal pay, and to value things typically or traditionally female. Above all, perhaps, a crucial modernist feminist political aim is to improve women's lives.

As we know, postmodernist feminists do not work with the idea that the important political act is to discover the truth of the subject of

woman. Instead they spend time on showing how woman is represented. The politics of this practice is in showing some of the effects
of the varied representations of woman and women. Because postmodern feminists are not working with a foundational epistemology
(there is no 'real', 'one' truth out there waiting to be discovered),
they do not spend any time looking for it. Instead they exert their ener-
gies into interrogating all the ways in which truth claims are made
about women – feminist or otherwise. Because *all* theories and practices
are involved in the exercise of power – *all* theories and practices need
to be constantly challenged and destabilised. Again, crucially, this
includes feminist theories and practices.

Going on this brief summary of the arguments made in this book, we
could certainly argue that there *is* a gulf between modernist and postmodernist feminisms. The postmodern feminist insistence on destabilisation *especially* in the context of identities – particularly that of
woman – together with their eschewal of the idea that the truth
(about women) can be proved, seems to indicate a stark contrast
with modernist feminisms.

## Different ideas about theory

However, one of the problems in any discussion about a gulf between
modernist and postmodernist feminisms revolves around the issue of
comparing like with like – or perhaps more accurately comparing
*unlike* with *unlike*. It may very well be the case that modernist and postmodernist feminists have rather different understandings or beliefs
about the role and use of theory, for example. Radical and socialist
feminist theories are centrally concerned with liberating women from
the oppressive structures of patriarchy and capitalism however they
are manifested, for instance in the realm of the material or the psychic.
And generally all modernist feminists share a number of theoretical
characteristics, namely, a normative commitment to women's emancipation (or equality in the case of liberal feminism), a scientific commitment to the explanation of women's oppression (or inequality), and a
practical commitment to social transformation (McClure, 1992: 349).
Each of these modernist feminist theories identified features (gender
roles or patriarchy for example) that were amenable to causal explanation and subsequent change. The purpose of theory for liberals, radicals
and socialists is therefore about offering both explanations for the
injustices and suggestions for practical action to change things.

Postmodern feminists argue that the underlying project of modernist
feminisms in terms of striving for a unified, coherent, universally useful

theory based on identity politics is misconceived. Postmodern feminists question all the concepts readily used by 1970s feminists including, 'causes', 'theory' and 'women's oppression/inequality'. They dispute the project of searching for causes, the claim that there is a cause or causes which can be discovered and used for explanatory purposes. Instead of asking 'why?', postmodern feminists prefer to ask 'how?' Modernist feminists think of theory as an explanatory tool and guide to action; for postmoderns, theory is a method to interrogate the process and effects of knowledge-making. Women's oppression, a phrase so often used by radical and socialist feminists in particular, is not especially liked by postmodern feminists. First, the assumption is questioned that oppression can be identified objectively; and second, it is questioned whether all women, everywhere, were oppressed. As such, one of the aims of postmodern feminist theory is to destabilise the assumptions of modernist feminisms, especially as the latter have been said to be 'virtually useless' (Gatens, 1992: 120) and 'anachronistic' (Coole, 1994: 129). Does all this supply us with supporting evidence of a gulf between modernist and postmodernist feminisms?

## Different ideas about politics

Let us look at another area of difference – in the realm of politics. Postmodern feminists argue that modernist feminists understand feminist politics as activities and practices that fundamentally require an 'ontologically grounded feminist subject' (Butler and Scott, 1992: xiv). Postmodern feminists regard this insistence as an act of authority which has the (unintended) consequence of setting limits on the political possibilities. According to postmodernists, modernist feminists decide in advance what women are (or should be) and then proceed to base their explanations and prescriptions on this. Contrary to this, postmodern feminists have no wish to define women but also claim that the uncertainty that results from the abandonment of the belief in the certainty of the subject does not have to lead to a situation where no political action can be taken. Indeed, postmodern feminists argue that the indeterminacy of the category of woman is not a cause for dismay, 'it is what *makes* feminism' (Riley, 1988: 114).

Postmodern feminists argue that modernist feminists both misunderstand what it means to deconstruct the category of woman and have a narrow view of what counts as political and of power. Modernist feminists appear to think that claiming woman is the effect of discourse, language and power and that the work of feminists is to expose that, is not political (or not political enough). They argue that it is necessary to discuss real women's lives and not to remain at the level of the text or language. However, postmodern feminists claim that to discuss the representation of women *is* to discuss the real. To show, for example, how women are represented and constructed in and by language is an enormously important political act. On the other hand the modernist feminist attempt to reify the category of woman into an artificial unity is more an authoritarian act than a politically emancipatory one.

As we can see, postmodern feminists conceptualise politics and power in rather different ways to modernist feminists. For those influenced by Foucault, power is seen to be exercised rather than possessed and is not always repressive (Sawicki, 1991: 21). What this implies is that postmodern feminists are not specifically concerned to battle against putatively powerful monolithic entities such as patriarchy or capitalism, or to see women as victims of oppressive forces. Instead, power is conceptualised as rather more dispersed and fluid and even a productive force, as where there is power there is resistance (ibid.).

But as postmodern feminists will argue, none of this implies that they cannot speak about women, or 'do' politics. Instead it means that essentialist and reified versions of women are exposed. In the words of our quintessential postmodern feminist, the deconstruction of woman is meant to 'release the category into a future of multiple significations . . . [and] expand the possibilities of what it means to be a woman . . . and to give it play as a site where unanticipated meanings might come to bear' (Butler, 1995: 50). Postmodern feminists would argue that discussing representations of women has great political potential as it leaves open the question of what woman is and 'how it would be possible to do justice to women' (Elam, 1994: 31). Trying to close down these questions, whether by feminists or misogynists, has been problematic for women. Uncertainty (about what woman is) is not an obstacle to action nor a theoretical bar to political praxis (ibid.). Too much certainty and false beliefs offering 'easy answers' merely camouflage contradictions and complexities.

On the other hand, the political demands of modernist feminisms are familiar. Liberal feminists have campaigned and lobbied for a variety of things, including the inclusion of women into education, the professions and party politics. Liberal feminists have historically based their claims on the rights of women (as equal, reasoning beings) and the injustice of unfair discrimination. In the context of feminist theory, especially with regard to its viability and practice, liberal feminists do not think of reproductive technologies, for example, as either inherently bad or good. Instead they see them as an inevitable result of scientific and technological progress. The important thing is to use them to women's best advantage, especially in the context of reproduction, where women are at a 'natural' disadvantage.

Radical feminists have not ignored the utility of legislation but their ultimate goal is the creation of a woman-culture which eradicates patriarchy and allows women's real interests to flourish. Such aims are based on the belief that women have been used primarily to meet the needs of patriarchy. In the context of reproductive technologies, this has resulted in a fear about the potential and actual uses of such technologies to abuse women's bodies in new ways and further remove the control of giving birth away from women and into the hands of men. For radical feminists, the political project entails both educating women about the 'facts' and resisting the continued development of these technologies. Socialist feminists are concerned to eliminate the sexual division of labour and expose the capitalist and patriarchal ideologies that construct subjectivities. In the context of reproductive technologies, the political project involves a theoretical commitment to construct a systematic explanation for the policies and practices of these technologies and a practical commitment to ensure increased democratic control on the part of those going through the experience of them.

## Room for doubt? Different gulfs?

It seems to be clear that there are significant differences between 1970s and 1990s feminisms. However, one might also argue that the significant unity between 1970s modernist feminisms has been exaggerated. We could argue that there is a *more* significant gulf between liberal feminism *and* radical and socialist feminism, rather than between the three and postmodern feminism. The epistemological challenges of both radical and socialist feminisms, and the structural analyses they put forward, is radically different to that of liberal feminism. Additionally we might say that the epistemological work of both radical and socialist feminists is just as significant an influence on postmodern feminism's conceptualisation of knowledge as is postmodernism – giving an impression of significant links or at least threads between 1970s and 1990s feminisms. The social construction of meaning with regard to women's lives and behaviours instigated by radical feminist approaches and the historical materialist approach of socialist feminism leads to a radically different understanding of things such as reproductive technologies than that offered by liberal feminists. For socialist and radical feminists this implies understanding the social and cultural construction of motherhood as a prerequisite to analysing reproductive technologies.

Our attention might be drawn to yet more similarities. The post-modern shunning of structurally based analysis might align it with the more pragmatic, piecemeal approach of liberal feminism; its perception of theory as everyday practice bears a similarity to radical feminism; and its emphasis on the constructive nature of meaning and reality arguably links it with the historical materialist approaches of socialist feminism. Clearly, a concern with the politics of feminism links all four theories. Furthermore, when we think the theories through practices, the differences seem to matter less than is implied by the theoretical gulf.

### Thinking again through practice

Let us think for a moment how the idea of a gulf works alongside examples from practice. Take the example of Image 4.1.

> *I am 40 years of age and for the past 10 years have been pursuing infertility treatment. This has led to three miscarriages and four unsuccessful IVF treatments. We have spent all our savings and most of our available energy. I am weary of traipsing round infertility clinics, of examinations, injections, operations, treatments. I am weary of failure, and empty years, and feel that it is time to stop and try to somehow accept that we will never have children. However, I don't know what to do next. I always thought that I would be a mother. Now it is not to be. The house is still empty. In the past 10 years I have sat in a dead-end job waiting to become pregnant. Now I feel I have nothing – not even a career to throw myself into. I don't know how to go forward. I don't know how to put a life together, that has meaning and purpose, and happiness, that doesn't include children. Please help me.*
> *(Letter to Private Lives section of the* Guardian, *5 April, 1999: 17)*

In Chapter 4 I read this tale using typically postmodern feminist questions and ideas. This led to suggestions that this woman could be described as in a 'moment' of resistance and deconstruction – that is resisting and deconstructing the category of womanhood that she seemingly had 'failed' to fulfil successfully. Of course, the postmodern feminist intention is *not* to provide an emancipatory or practical set of suggestions to this woman in order to make her feel better or empowered in her specific circumstances. Instead the postmodern aim is to read this story in numerous ways and to deconstruct the meanings within it and to trace the ways in which these meanings have developed. For example, I introduced a discussion about the 'desperateness' with regard to childlessness that was evident in the letter. I suggested that the sense of 'failure' seemingly experienced by this woman was an area that could be explored with the idea of thinking about and deconstructing a specific category of woman – that is mother (or 'failed' mother in this case).

For postmodernist feminists working without the desire to 'prove' or destroy patriarchy or capitalism, for example, these feminists are in some ways 'freed up' to pursue a huge variety of interrogations. These might include asking why feminists are so interested in questions about motherhood – what effect might such a focus have? Too easy an acceptance of heterosexist logic perhaps? Additionally the postmodern concern with the construction of legitimate subjects leads them to analyse all such constructions – 'illegitimate' foetuses for example.

Pursuing the idea that thinking theory through practice casts doubt on the claim that there is a significant gulf between 1970s and 1990s feminisms, I want to look at this image from a modernist feminist agenda. Whatever the theoretical differences between liberal, socialist and radical feminisms, it is generally the case that these feminists are very keen on exposing how distress in a woman's life is frequently the result of sexist injustice or oppression. This is done with a view to making some sort of practical demand to improve that woman's life and women's lives in general. This can lead to a wide variety of modernist feminist readings. For example, liberal feminists may question the 'over-attachment' to the idea that being a mother is the key to a woman's fulfilment. Perhaps this woman might have had a more fulfilling life had she become a mountain climber or a stockbroker. A socialist feminist might suggest that if less money were channelled into profits for a small number or people, or into typically masculinist pursuits such as the arms race or the space race, more money might be available for research into infertility, perhaps leading to an earlier and more successful resolution to this woman's problem. A radical feminist, although sympathising with this woman's desire to be a mother, might prefer to document the waste and pain of her life in the pursuit of attempting to satisfy the demands of the heterosexual and patriarchal nuclear family.

This is a brief snapshot version of possible modernist feminist readings of this particular story. Does this amount to something significantly different to postmodern feminist readings? Does this thinking of theory through practice give us more evidence of a gulf between modernist and postmodernist feminisms?

Clearly the commitment to proving injustice and working towards emancipatory or just ends for women using foundational ideas about subjects and knowledges distinguishes modernist feminisms from post-modernist feminisms. And clearly the postmodern feminist eschewal of the emancipatory potential of modernist feminist identity politics sets them apart from modernist feminists. But are there also significant similarities – or at least ways of thinking about these two bodies of feminist thought which go against the idea that there is a huge gulf between them? For example, is it not the case that each group of feminists is questioning what it means to be a mother and why the varied circumstances surrounding motherhood seem to 'box' women in one way or another?

To be sure, the postmodern feminist practice of not 'stopping the questioning' or endless deconstruction and not even stopping at gender and/or women might make a difference to modernist feminisms. But is the difference significant? Does it amount to an unbridgeable gulf, especially when we think the theories through into practice? Let us look at another of the images I used earlier – Image 4.3 – and think it through both modernist and postmodern feminisms.

> In 1994 . . . 19 year old Kawana Michelle Ashley . . . shot herself in the stomach . . . She was delivered by an emergency Caesarean section of a baby girl. She [the baby] died April 11. Ashley was charged with third degree murder and manslaughter: newspapers reported allegations that she killed her '6-month-old-fetus' 'by shooting herself in the womb'.
>
> (Squier, 1996: 515)

Postmodern feminists might use this image to trace a story of some of the effects of contemporary reproductive technologies, even though we do not know if this particular woman has personally experienced the use of reproductive technologies. The postmodern story told shows us how the practice of technologies such as ultrasound may have created new knowledge about the inside of a pregnant woman's body, leading to new knowledges about the foetus – altering or intro-ducing new beliefs about rights to the privileges of identity that being a subject allows (or disallows). This has opened up new ways for those with particular authority in society (such as the medical profes-sion and the judiciary) both to give the foetus rights and to balance those rights against the rights of the mother. In the story of Kawana Ashley, this has culminated in the redescription of an 'attempted suicide' into a 'murder'. Such a redefinition obviously has huge practical consequences, especially in the everyday life of Kawana Ashley.

Would a modernist feminist have a drastically different reading of the story about Kawana Ashley? They might argue that the postmodernist feminist approach is too removed or too distanced. To be sure, a radical or socialist feminist activist group might organise a public campaign to demonstrate against the attempt to criminalise Kawana Ashley. But who is to say that a postmodern feminist would not take part in such a demonstration? My aim in this book is not to suggests that feminist writers should or do remain rigidly in their theoretical camps professionally, personally and publicly, or to work out what individual feminists might or might not do. The point, as I said in the introduction, is to use the images of seemingly radically opposed feminists (such as Andrea Dworkin and Judith Butler) to help us think about what different feminisms allow, enable or inspire us to do.

But still, a modernist feminist might argue that the sense of distance or abstract theorising in typically postmodern analyses is not very empowering or enabling for women. This indicates an important area of difference between modernist and postmodernist feminisms underpinning the modernist feminist claim that postmodernist feminisms are apolitical. For example, in the context of the story of Kawana Ashley, a modernist feminist might argue that spending time and effort discussing how visualising the foetus (through the technology of ultrasound) constructs new subjects is of little use to Kawana Ashley. This woman must surely be in a terrible state having shot herself, 'killed' her foetus and now having to face trial. Surely what is needed ranges from practical support at the very least, to political action aimed at transforming the biased and cruel legal system and patriarchal structures overall at best?

Let us pursue this potential area of significant difference between modernist and postmodernist feminisms. The argument is that postmodern feminist approaches are too far removed from reality and real needs, leading to the claim that they lack a satisfactory politics or that they are simply apolitical. Think of Image 4.4.

> *Allow me to tell you, dear human brethren, that I am the fruit of a unique mutation. Even in my original cell phase, I knew exactly where I was going. Can one even maintain that I was 'conceived' in the true sense of the term? I doubt it. Had I not always existed? . . .*

*I am living proof that the fetus is not man's initial state, but his total state, after which it is all downhill . . . I am my dearest enigma to myself: I never tire of trying to solve myself. Why, I can affirm that I've come a long way, I'm fine today – to quote dear old Hegel, 'Knowledge as the self-conceiving self' – if you catch my drift. My peculiarity? I am only a brain, a giant intellectual apparatus.*
                    *(Bruckner, 1994:79, quoted in Squier, 1996: 526)*

This is a science fiction story – an imagined tale. A modernist feminist keen on practical politics might claim that postmodern analysis of this story is an intellectual indulgence and of no use whatsoever in everyday, practical situations. But surely one can argue that the postmodern foray into the imaginary is not very different to radical and socialist feminist reworkings and re-imaginings of reality? Redescribing reality or the everyday is something of a hallmark of radical feminist work. Does it matter which routes we take to open up and explore how the stories about what is 'right' or 'just' or 'true' become real? And, as many radical feminists would claim, science fiction stories in the realm of reproductive technologies are often not dissimilar to contemporary (or past) practices. The image of a writhing and screaming Zelda (from Image 4.5) – a 'caricature of femininity' – will not seem a million miles away from many women's experiences in the throes of childbirth attached to machines which make the pain of labour more difficult to bear.

Of course the idea that a Zelda-like experience is not that far removed from reality might be more easily believed than the story of Louis – a foetus apparently with agency of his own. But think about the recent reporting of the birth of a baby boy who had 'managed to create an "artificial" womb of his own' (*Daily Mail*, 1999: 2). A woman who conceived triplets, two of which gestated in her womb (two girls), but the third, a boy, 'burst' its way out of the fallopian tube in which it had started to develop and then 'created' its own womb-like sac. All three babies were born alive and well enough in the circumstances (Caesarean delivery at 29 weeks) – indeed, the boy was reported to be doing 'better than his sisters'. The image that the boy created his own 'womb-like sac' certainly seems to award agency to this child.

It might still be the case that modernist feminists would argue that deconstructing the fictional and the imaginary is not enough, and that a more practical, 'hands-on' politics is called for if feminist politics is to really have an effect. But again perhaps the issue here is not so much located in the presumed political *inadequacies* of postmodern feminisms but rather around the question of the *different* approaches that these bodies of feminism are interested in.

This perhaps casts further doubt on the claims about a paradigmatic shift between 1970s and 1990s feminisms, especially when we think the theories through into practice. Another example is the Foucauldian analysis of the example of prenatal screening, which presents it as a classic case of biopower in that it disciplines and regulates female bodies (Sawicki, 1991). This conclusion is not totally dissimilar to some radical and socialist feminist analyses of prenatal screening. However, the essence of the claim made by some contemporary feminists, for example Barrett and Phillips (1992: 2), about the putative shift from 1970s feminisms to 1990s feminisms – the gulf – is that it is the *assumptions* rather than *conclusions* which are radically overturned. If the conclusions of feminist theorising have not been radically overturned, where are the effects of this debate about a gulf to be found? Perhaps we should ask what some of the effects of the debate between feminisms have been within feminisms themselves.

## 'Recovering' (the gulf) between feminisms?

In a recent discussion on the UK radio programme *Woman's Hour*, two British feminists (Beatrix Campbell and Rosalind Coward) were discussing the contemporary and future relevance of feminism.[1] This discussion took place in the context of the publication of Rosalind Coward's book *Sacred Cows: Is Feminism Relevant to the New Millennium?* (1999). Towards the end of the discussion Rosalind Coward described herself as a 'recovering feminist', implying that she had 'recovered' from her belief in the continuing relevance of 1970s feminisms.

This idea of 'recovery' in the context of a gulf between 1970s and 1990s feminisms can be thought about in several ways. One idea would be of a layering over of the older feminisms so that they become buried and any sense of their use is lost. This version of (re)covering (over and over) would fit in well with the idea that 1970s feminisms are 'virtually useless'. On the other hand the idea of recovering could give an impression of building up stronger and stronger layers or linked threads so that ideas and beliefs about feminist theories and practices drew strength from each other. This way of thinking about recovering does not fit very well with the idea that there are huge theoretical and political incompatibilities between 1970s and 1990s feminisms. A third way of thinking about recovery is in the context of convalescing from an illness or (feminist?) madness – which is the sense that Rosalind Coward seems to imply! Perhaps recovery in this sense refers to a return to 'sane' and conventional ways of thinking!

In a quite significant way it seems that the argument that there *is* a significant gulf between 1970s and 1990s such that the older feminisms are described as anachronistic, results in the manifestation of the first version of 'recovery' described above – that is, a burying and loss of the older feminisms. There are several serious problems with this view. First, it seems unnecessarily and unpleasantly divisive. It has been the task of some postmodern feminists to criticise modernist feminisms for 'policing' feminist categories of thought because they appear to present themselves as the official authority on what women should do or not do (Haraway, 1991: 156). Yet imposing the idea that there is a gulf between 1970s and 1990s feminisms and branding 1970s feminisms as out of date is surely a clear example of policing categories of feminist thought?

A second and linked point concerns the claim that the more traditional feminisms are anachronistic. The imagery of linear time and space suggested by the word 'anachronism' seems at odds with the postmodern eschewal of stories of historical lineage. It would seem more in keeping with postmodern strategies to *be* anachronistic as a strategy of destabilisation. The *Chambers Essential English Dictionary* defines anachronism as 'an instance of placing something in a time earlier or later than the period to which it belongs – such as describing an aircraft carrier at Trafalgar' (1973: 17). The anachronistic arrival of an aircraft carrier at Trafalgar would certainly have had devastatingly, destabilising results. The 'locking' of theories such as radical or socialist feminism in a specific time period with the accompanying implication of the arrival of a more progressive form of contemporary feminism is surely an example of policing feminisms. It both encourages a sense of progressive lineage (feminisms *after* postmodernism?) as well as not allowing for the changes and developments in these theories. The complexities of contemporary socialist feminism surely cannot lead it to be described as anachronistic.

Furthermore, the construction of a gulf between modernist and postmodernist feminisms seems radically at odds with the postmodern claim to want to destabilise dualisms; surely the feminist modernist/postmodernist divide is a prime example of a dualism to be destabilised rather than reinforced? Even more than this, one can argue that the feminist modernist/postmodernist dualism is a prime example of the illusion of such a divide. Modernist feminisms paradigmatically challenge Enlightenment thought by rejecting its epistemology as fundamentally male biased (Hekman, 1992: 1–2). Yet at the same time modernist feminism has looked to the methods of modernism on which to base a politics of feminism. As such, there is a profound ambiguity in feminism: it challenges modernist epistemology but is located in the emancipatory impulses of modernism. So in a sense *all* feminisms are in an anomalous position vis-à-vis the modernist/postmodernist debate. The idea of a gulf seems inadequate to capture this intriguing ambiguity. Instead it encourages a policing and disciplining set of strategies.

## Policing feminist stories

> What matters is not the variety of stories . . . but the power of these narratives to structure practice.
>
> (Birke, 1998: 217)

It may be the case that many feminists of a modernist mind-set are 'radically disenchanted' with a postmodern world (Brown, 1995: 43) and fear a loss of the ability to 'do' feminist politics in practically meaningful ways. It also may be the case that many postmodern feminists cannot intellectually accept modernist political projects that appear to go against their stated intentions by boxing women into more and more categories continually denying differences. But I seriously question the desire to 'do battle' amongst these feminisms, resulting in each decrying the other's utility.

In positing a gulf between modernist and postmodern feminisms, Barrett and Phillips, Gatens and Coole have arguably constructed their own authoritative taxonomy which has the effect of denying both the continued usefulness of modernist feminisms and the debt that postmodern feminisms owe to the former. If we think for a moment about the utility issue, let me supply two examples in the context of political effectiveness and epistemology. Liberal feminism's piecemeal, pragmatic approach may harbour the dangers of relying on rights-based theories, but as a practical strategy in the context of political systems that work on the principle of the rights of individuals, it offers a way of manoeuvring through that system in ways that deconstructing fictional texts do not. Radical feminism's fatalistic and sometimes divisive approach limits its claim to political effectiveness. But its reconceptualisation of knowledge is arguably a prerequisite to postmodern feminism's own radical reconceptualisation of epistemology. In both cases, what counts as 'success' or an 'effective strategy' is different. On the question of usefulness, if some women find more traditional feminisms of use to them, is it not an exercise of authority to declare these feminisms useless?

Similarly, feminist arguments that postmodern approaches stray too far into the realm of the fictional are perhaps also an exercise in making authoritarian judgements and policing feminisms. The 'advocacy of avant-garde practices narrow[s] and isolate[s] political struggles to a form of discursive engagement specific to intellectuals . . . ushering the privileged Western intellectual in through a side door' (Stabile, 1994: 146). I take this to mean that the postmodern use of rhetoric, metaphor and imaginative devices is really a form of intellectually indulgent play and therefore of little use in changing the material lives of women. But this point clearly depends on understandings about the nature of *politics*. For many modernist feminists, politics cannot remain in the realm of creative intellectual practices. But surely this too is being authoritative and perhaps underestimates the seriousness of 'releasing the play of writing'? It is not insignificant that books get burned (such as the destruction of 'degenerate' literature by the Nazis; or the public burning of Salman Rushdie's *The Satanic Verses*) and that science fiction dystopian futures often portray a world in which words are both dangerous and scarce; in the case of Margaret Attwood's *Handmaid's Tale* (1986) the word-game *Scrabble* is depicted as having become a pornographic and secret activity. Words and stories can be powerful tools in creating meaning and there- fore 'reality'. Changing the story can change the 'reality' but in order to do that, 'if we are imprisoned by language, then escape from that prison-house requires language poets' (Haraway, 1991: 245). And poets often produce work that initially seems meaningless with the words jumbled up and presented in 'strange' ways. But it is arguably at the edge of 'sense' that new stories can be made. I would argue that there is certainly a place for postmodern feminist interpretations of what counts as political. The problem is more accurately located in the hierarchical arranging of levels of the political.

## Riding with feminist gulfs and waves

There are indeed different ways of doing feminism, but the entrench- ment of feminist work in academic institutions has arguably encour- aged a stereotypical academic approach which involves building reputations on the basis of finding fault with the work of others. One might be tempted to regard this as a paradigmatically masculinist approach, which is not to say that women do not do it. In the context of issues to do with feminism, women and gender, there is a lot at stake. 'Feminist theorizing is a *writing* to save lives' (Clough, 1994: 6). Dismissal of the path-breaking work of radical feminists, for example, as either anachronistic or virtually useless seems bizarre. Similarly, evoking 'commonsense' comparisons such as the effectiveness of the politics of the women's liberation movement versus the practical useful-ness of poetic perusals of 'how women get said', both misses the point and invokes an unhelpful level of acrimony. It is possible to change one's life by reading poetry, or thinking in a poetic manner, in ways that are as fundamental as the provision of legislation or more informa-tion. Furthermore, 'to lose the sense of what has gone before [in terms of feminist work] is to be burdened with the task of constantly reinvent-ing the wheel' (Whelehan, 1995: 247). What is 'virtually useless' for contemporary feminist theories and practices is to make *non*-sense of both what has gone before and what might be in the future.

To return to a question I have used several times throughout this book: 'In the face of what is, what should we do?' (Price, 1997: 34). If we asked Andrea Dworkin and Judith Butler this question, what might their answers be? Of course it would depend on what they take 'what is' to mean as well as what it means to 'do' something. But they might agree that they want to make women's lives better – but have radically different ways of approaching that. There clearly *are* some significant differences between 1970s and 1990s feminisms, most obviously in the realm of theory, but I would argue that the differences do not have to imply dismissals of either group of feminisms by the other.

How might we think of or use feminism – in theory and in practice – in the twenty-first century? There is surely no consensus on this ques-tion – and neither should there be. But as we move through the twenty-first century and popular (best-selling) feminism turns its focus towards men as the 'new victims of gender',[2] then perhaps one crucial way to 'recover' feminisms is to be found in recovering feminisms from the intolerances of other feminisms – as well as the more traditional 'others'.

## Notes

1 *Woman's Hour*, BBC Radio 4, 7 July 1999.
2 Fay Weldon quoted in Coward, 1999: 72. See also many of the arguments in Coward, 1999 and Faludi, 1999.

# Glossary of medical terms

**Alphafetoprotein/AFP**  A protein present in the blood of the human foetus or unborn child. Traces of this protein in the mother's blood may indicate a spinal defect (see Sutton, 1990: 198).

**Amniocentesis**  This is a well-established and widely available method for prenatal diagnosis (see Kingston, 1989: 1370). The test, which is usually carried out around the sixteenth week of pregnancy, involves extracting a small sample of the amniotic fluid via the abdomen using a fine spinal needle. Ultrasound is used to locate the amniotic fluid and placenta in order that the procedure can be carried out with precision. Once enough fluid has been collected, it is sent to the laboratory to be analysed. The fluid obtained may be analysed in three ways: the measurement of proteins, analysis of the chromosomal constitution of the cultured cells and biochemical analysis (see Crawfurd, 1988: 504). For example, once the foetal cells have been cultured, the chromosomal make-up of the foetus can be examined, and chromosomal abnormalities, such as Down's Syndrome, can be diagnosed. The sex of the foetus can also be confirmed in this way. Neural tube defects are diagnosed by measuring the concentration of alphafetoprotein which is raised in the presence of neural tube defects. The results of the analyses take from seven days up to four weeks (see Sutton, 1990: 20).

**Amniotic fluid**  The fluid surrounding the foetus within the amniotic sac (see Sutton, 1990: 198).

**Chromosomes**  Chain-like microscopic bodies in the nucleus or centre of cells which contain the genes or biological bases of heredity. The normal number of chromosomes in humans is 46. They come in pairs: 23 of paternal origin and 23 of maternal origin (see Sutton, 1990: 200).

**Chorionic Villus Sampling (CVS)**   Alternatively known as chorion biopsy, this is a fairly new technique which was pioneered in the Soviet Union, China and Scandinavia in the 1970s (see Jackson and Wapner, 1993). Early in pregnancy, the embryo is encased in a membrane (chorion) from which hairline wisps of tissue, known as villi, protrude. A fragment of the villi is extracted, either transcervically or transabdominally (the latter as in amniocentesis), which is then sent to the laboratory for testing. The advantage of this test, over amniocentesis, is that it can be done in the first trimester (first three months) of pregnancy. Results can be achieved at about the tenth week of pregnancy as opposed to the twentieth week in the case of amniocentesis. Results can be obtained in as little as two hours but usually within seven days (see Jackson and Wapner, 1993: 50). CVS was initially developed in China to detect the sex of the foetus. In 1975, the Chinese examined 100 cases, 30 pregnancies were terminated, 29 of them female foetuses (Tietung Hospital, 1975). The following investigations can be done with CVS: foetal sexing, chromosome analysis, biochemistry, DNA analysis. The test can pick up the same conditions as amniocentesis except that the level of alphafetoprotein cannot be measured and thus neural tube defects cannot be detected. There are no figures available at the moment on the prevalence of CVS in England and Wales, but in 1983 the technique was used to investigate 240 pregnancies world-wide. By 1992 that figure had increased to 80,000 (see Jackson and Wapner, 1993: 47).

**Cordocentesis**   This test involves taking a sample of foetal blood by inserting a hollow needle through the mother's abdomen into the umbilical vein. This is a procedure requiring high skills and is therefore usually only practised in the largest teaching hospitals. As it involves the introduction of a smaller instrument than fetoscopy, this technique is less invasive and so safer (see Sutton, 1990: 35). As it is generally used for the same reasons as fetoscopy, it is rapidly becoming the preferred blood-sampling technique (see Sutton, 1990: 35).

**Down's Syndrome**   Caused by an error in chromosome formation, causing varying levels of disability. It is associated with congenital heart disease and decreased life expectancy together with varying degrees of mental handicap (see Sutton, 1990: 201).

**Embryo**   Commonly, the early stages of development before recognisable human features are formed, at about eight weeks or so (see Sutton, 1990: 202).

**Eugenics** The science of the improvement of the human species by genetic means, championed by Sir Francis Galton (1822–1911), who proposed the idea of improving physical and mental characterisics by selective parenthood. It was the basis of the compulsory sterilisation laws passed in many countries in the early twentieth century and the Nazi 'racial hygiene' programme. *Negative Eugenics* refers to decreasing the propagation of the 'handicapped' or 'defective'. The term is used today to describe selective abortion of foetuses. The term *positive eugenics* refers to increasing the propagation of 'desirable' human types. In medical science, it denotes an approach whereby genetic disorders can be remedied or averted (for example, gene therapy). Selective pronatalism is a form of positive eugenics.

**Foetus (fetus)** The developing embryo which has achieved recognisable human features, usually referring to a gestational age of 8–40 weeks (see Sutton, 1990: 199).

**Fetoscopy** This covers a number of procedures which involve direct examination of the foetus or foetal blood or tissue. A fetoscope, a fine fibre-optic telescope, is passed through the abdomen into the uterus so that the foetus can be seen. It is performed under local anaesthetic when the woman is between 16 and 20 weeks pregnant (see Sutton, 1990: 21). It is usually undertaken in situations where there is doubt about the diagnosis from ultrasound and the gestation is such that X-rays are not possible (early on in the pregnancy when greatest harm can be done to the developing foetus by X-rays). Fetoscopy provides a narrow field of view, so only a small part of the foetus can be seen at any one time. The diagnosis of structural abnormalities with this technique is limited. It is often used to detect sickle cell disease and haemophilia (see Sutton, 1990: 32).

**In Vitro Fertilisation (IVF)** This is also colloquially known as the 'test-tube baby' technology. It refers to the technique of mixing a woman's eggs with sperm in a small dish or test tube in the laboratory to allow fertilisation to ocur. Once the eggs are fertilised and have divided, one or more of the fertilised eggs are replaced in the woman's uterus (womb) through the cervix.

**Neural tube defects/NTDs** Neural tube defects affect the spine and/or the brain. They account for about 50 per cent of all abnormalities at birth. They include anencephaly – always fatal at or before birth – and spina bifida, in which some of the vertebrae might be missing and some spinal cord tissue may protrude outside the body. The latter is called an open neural tube defect; if tissue does not protrude, it is defined as closed. About one baby in 1,000 is born with anencephaly in England and Wales every year and one baby in 500 with spina bifida (see Spiby, 1987: 11).

**Prenatal screening/diagnosis**   The terms 'screening' and 'diagnosis' are often used interchangeably, although strictly there is a difference between them. Screening tests establish the criteria on which a judgement will be made about proceeding to a diagnostic test and ultimately to decisions about action. But generally, 'prenatal diagnosis is a process' not one single event (Green, 1990: 4). Screening tests and diagnostic tests are all part of the same procedure; it is difficult to draw a boundary line between them (see Reid, 1990: 303). If an initial screening test indicates that no further action needs to be taken, that is no diagnostic tests need to be carried out because an abnormality is not suspected, the screening test is still part of the process. As such, 'the definition of screening is based largely on the fact that it is the *purpose* for which a procedure is carried out that qualifies it as screening. It is not the test itself that qualifies it as a screening test' (Wald, 1984: 2; emphasis added). Examples of diagnostic tests which are usually divided into invasive and non-invasive tests (see Sutton, 1990: 19) include:

| | |
|---|---|
| *Invasive, mother only* | Maternal Serum Alphafetoprotein testing |
| | Combined maternal blood test |
| *Invasive, both foetus and mother* | Amniocentesis |
| | Chorion biopsy (or Chorion Villus Sampling) |
| | Fetoscopy |
| | Cordocentesis |
| *Non-invasive* | Ultrasound scanning |
| | Radiography |

**Ultrasound**   This is a well-established prenatal screening and diagnostic procedure, indeed it has been described as 'the standard method for the detection of foetal congenital abnormalities' (Sabbagha, 1993: 91). The technique involves bombarding the body with high-frequency sound waves which are bounced back off different organs and body spaces according to their density. The reflected waves are used to create a computerised picture on a television screen from which judgements can be made about the status of the foetus (see Docker, 1992: 69). For example, ultrasound can determine gestational age, foetal death, and identify multiple pregnancies. It establishes the position of the placenta and any growths or abnormalities in the shape of a woman's uterus which may obstruct delivery (see Sutton, 1990: 21). It can sometimes determine the sex of the foetus. In the most skilled hands, the best equipment available can reveal the internal anatomy of the foetus in great detail, so that many malformations can be diagnosed. It is also possible to measure blood flow in the major foetal and uterine vessels (see Docker, 1992: 77).

# References

Adams, A. (1994) *Reproducing the Womb: Images of Childbirth in Science, Feminist Theory, and Literature*, Ithaca: Cornell University Press.

Alcoff, L. (1997) 'The Politics of Postmodern Feminism Revisited', *Cultural Critique*, 36: 5–27.

Amos, V. and Parmar, P. (1984) 'Challenging Imperial Feminism', *Feminist Review*, 17: 3–20.

Arditti, R., Klein, D. and Minden, S. (eds) (1985) *Test-Tube Women: What Future For Motherhood?*, London: Pandora.

Atkinson, D. (1997) *Funny Girls: Cartooning for Equality*, London: Penguin Books.

Attwood, M. (1986) *The Handmaid's Tale*, New York: Random House.

Baines, E. (1983) *The Birth Machine*, London: The Women's Press.

Barr, M. (1988) 'Blurred Generic Conventions: Pregnancy and Power in Feminist Science Fiction', *Reproductive and Genetic Engineering*, 1, 2: 167–174.

Barrett, Michele (1992) 'Words and Things: Materialism and Method in Contemporary Feminist Analysis', in M. Barrett and A. Phillips (eds) *Destabilizing Theory: Contemporary Feminist Debates*, Oxford: Polity Press, 201–219.

Barrett, M. and Phillips, A. (eds) (1992) *Destabilizing Theory: Contemporary Feminist Debates*, Oxford: Polity Press.

Bell, D. and Klein, R. (1996) *Radically Speaking: Feminism Reclaimed*, London: Zed Books.

Benhabib, S. (1992) *Situating the Self: Gender, Community and Postmodernism in Contemporary Ethics*, London: Routledge.

Birke, L. (1998) 'The Broken Heart' in Margrit Shildrick and Janet Price (eds) *Vital Signs: Feminist Reconfigurations of the Bio/logical Body*, Edinburgh: Edinburgh University Press, 197–223.

Braidotti, R. (1987) 'Envy: Or with Your Brains and My Looks', in Alice Jardine and Paul Smith (eds) *Men in Feminism*, New York: Methuen.

Brock, D., Rodeck, C. and Ferguson-Smith, M. (eds) (1992) *Prenatal Diagnosis and Screening*, Edinburgh: Churchill Livingstone.

Brooks, A. (1997) *Postfeminisms. Feminisms, Cultural Theory and Cultural Forms*, London: Routledge.

Brown, W. (1995) *States of Injury*, Princeton: Princeton University Press.

Bruckner, P. (1994) *The Divine Child: A Novel of Prenatal Rebellion*, J. Neugroschel (trans.), Boston: Little Brown & Co.

Bryson, V. (1992) *Feminist Political Theory*, Basingstoke: Macmillan.

Butler, J. (1990) *Gender Trouble*, London: Routledge.

—— (1995) 'Contingent Foundations' in S. Benhabib *et al.*, *Feminist Contentions*, London: Routledge, 35–57.

Butler, J. and Scott, J. W. (eds) (1992) *Feminists Theorize the Political*, London: Routledge.

Cahoone, L. E. (1996) *From Modernism to Postmodernism: An Anthology*, Oxford: Basil Blackwell.

Chancer, L. S. (1998) *Reconcilable Differences*, Berkeley: University of California Press.

Chodorow, N. (1978) *The Reproduction of Mothering*, London: University of California Press.

Clough, P. T. (1994) *Feminist Thought*, Oxford: Blackwell.

Cohn, C. (1994) 'Wars, Wimps and Women: Talking Gender and Thinking War' in M. Cooke and A. Wollacott (eds) *Gendering War Talk*, Princeton: Princeton University Press, 227–248.

Coole, D. (1993) *Women in Political Theory*, London: Harvester Wheatsheaf.

—— (1994) 'Whither Feminisms?', *Political Studies* 42, 1: 128–134.

Corea, G. (1988) *The Mother Machine*, London: The Women's Press.

—— (1990) 'Women, Class and Genetic Engineering – The Effect of New Reproductive Technologies on all Women', in Jocelynne Scutt (ed.) *The Body Machine*, London, Merlin Press, 135–156.

Coward, R. (1999) *Sacred Cows: Is Feminism Relevant to the New Millennium?*, London: HarperCollins.

Crawfurd, M. d'A. (1988) 'Prenatal Diagnosis of Common Genetic Disorders', *The British Medical Journal*, 297: 502–506.

—— (1992), 'Medicolegal aspects – UK/Europe' in D. Brock, C. Rodeck and M. Ferguson-Smith (eds) *Prenatal Diagnosis and Screening*, Edinburgh: Churchill Livingstone, 755–759.

*Daily Mail*, 'Courage of the Mother who Risked her Life for her Triplets', 11 September 1999: 2.

Daly, M. (1979) *Gyn/Ecology: The Metaethics of Radical Feminism*, London: The Women's Press.

De Lauretis, T. (1984) *Alice Doesn't: Feminism, Semiotics and Cinema*, Bloomington: Indiana University Press.

Degener, T. (1990) 'Female Self-Determination between Feminist Claims and "Voluntary" Eugenics, between "Rights" and Ethics', *Issues in Reproductive and Genetic Engineering*, 3, 2: 87–99.

Derrida, J. (1976) *Of Grammatology*, trans. Gaytri Chakravorty Spivak. Baltimore: The Johns Hopkins University Press.

—— (1979) *Spurs: Nietzsche's Styles/Eperons: Les Styles de Nietzsche*, trans. Barbara Harlow. Chicago: The University of Chicago Press.

—— (1981) *Positions*, trans. Alan Bass. Chicago: The University of Chicago Press.

—— (1992) *Given Time: I. Counterfeit Money*, trans. Peggy Kamuf. Chicago: The University of Chicago Press.

Di Stefano, C. (1990) 'Dilemmas of Difference: Feminism, Modernity and Postmodernism', in L. J. Nicholson (ed.) *Feminism/Postmodernism*, London: Routledge, 63–82.

Docker, M. (1992) 'Ultrasound Imaging Techniques', in D. Brock, C. Rodeck and M. Ferguson-Smith (eds) *Prenatal Diagnosis and Screening*, Edinburgh: Churchill Livingstone, 69–81.

Donovan, J. (1988) *Feminist Theory: The Intellectual Traditions of American Feminism*, New York: Continuum.

Dworkin, A. (1983) *Right-wing Women*, London: The Women's Press.

—— (1989) *Pornography*, New York: Plume Books.

Eisenstein, Z. R. (1986) *The Radical Future of Liberal Feminism*, Boston: Northeastern University Press.

Elam, D. (1994) *Feminism and Deconstruction*, London: Routledge.

Faludi, S. (1999) *Stiffed: The Betrayal of Modern Man*, London: Chatto & Windus.

Farquhar, D. (1996) *The Other Machine: Discourse and Reproductive Technologies*, London: Routledge.

Farrant, W. (1985) 'Who's for Amniocentesis? The Politics of Prenatal Screening' in H. Homans (ed.) *The Sexual Politics of Reproduction*, Aldershot: Gower Publishing, 96–122.

Feder, E., Rawlinson, M. and Zakin, E. (1997), 'Introduction' in E. Feder, M. Rawlinson and E. Zakin (eds) *Derrida and Feminism*, London: Routledge, 1–6.

Ferguson, K. (1993) *The Man Question*, Berkeley: University of California Press.

Fitzsimons, L. (1997) 'Stop the Ladness!' in *Select*, October, no. 87, compiled by Lucy O'Brien.

Flax, J. (1990) *Thinking Fragments*, Berkeley: University of California Press.

—— (1993) *Disputed Subjects*, London: Routledge.

Foster, H. (1985) *Postmodern Culture*, London: Pluto Press.

Foster, P. (1989) 'Improving the Doctor/Patient Relationship: A Feminist Perspective', *Journal of Social Policy*, 18, 3: 337–361.

Foucault, M. (1967) *Madness and Civilization: A History of Insanity in the Age of Reason*, London: Tavistock.

—— (1972) *The Archaeology of Knowledge*, New York: Pantheon.

—— (1975) *The Birth of the Clinic: An Archaeology of Medical Perception*, New York: Vintage.

—— (1977) *Discipline and Punish: The Birth of the Prison*, Harmondsworth: Allen Lane.

—— (1979) *The History of Sexuality, Vol. 1: An Introduction*, Harmondsworth: Allen Lane.

Franklin, S. (1997) *Embodied Progress: A Cultural Account of Assisted Conception*, London: Routledge.

Fraser, N. and Nicholson, L. (1990) 'Social Criticism without Philosophy: An Encounter between Feminism and Postmodernism', in N. Fraser and L. Nicholson (eds) *Feminism/Postmodernism*, London: Routledge, 19–38.

Gardiner, J. K. (1992) 'Psychoanalysis and Feminism: An American Humanist's View', *Signs: Journal of Women in Culture and Society*, 17, 2: 437–454.

Gatens, M. (1992) 'Power, Bodies and Difference' in M. Barrett and A. Phillips (eds) *Destabilizing Theory: Contemporary Feminist Debates*, Oxford: Polity Press, 120–137.

Gilligan, C. (1982) *In a Different Voice*, Cambridge, Mass.: Harvard University Press.

Gilmore, D. H. and Aitken, D. A. (1989) 'Prenatal Screening' in M. J. Whittle and J. M. Connor (eds) *Prenatal Diagnosis in Obstetric Practice*, Oxford: Blackwell Scientific Publications, 22–32.

Grant, J. (1993) *Fundamental Feminism*, London: Routledge.

Green, J. M. (1990) *Calming or Harming? A Critical Review of Psychological Effects of Fetal Diagnosis on Pregnant Women*, London: Galton Institute.

Greer, G. (1970) *The Female Eunuch*, London: McGibbon & Kee.

—— (1999) *The Whole Woman*, London: Doubleday.

Gregg, R. (1995) *Pregnancy in a High-Tech Age: Paradoxes of Choice*, New York: New York University Press.

Griffin, S. (1980) *Women and Nature: The Roaring Inside Her*, New York: Harper Colophon.

Grimshaw, J. (1986) *Philosophy and Feminist Thinking*, Minneapolis: University of Minnesota Press.

*Guardian* (1999) letters in 'Private Lives' section, 5 April: 17.

Hansen, K. and Philipson, I. (eds) (1990) *Women, Class, and the Feminist Imagination*, Philadelphia: Temple University Press.

Haraway, D. (1991) *Simians, Cyborgs and Women: the Re-invention of Nature*, London: Free Association Books.

Harding, S. (1986) *The Science Question in Feminism*, Milton Keynes: Open University Press.

—— (1987) *Feminism and Methodology*, Milton Keynes: Open University Press.

—— (1991) *Whose Science? Whose Knowledge?*, Milton Keynes: Open University Press.

Hartsock, N. (1983a) 'The Feminist Standpoint: Developing the Ground for a Specifically Feminist Historical Materialism' in S. Harding and M. Hintikka (eds) *Discovering Reality*, Boston: D. Reidel, 283–310.

—— (1983b) *Money, Sex and Power*, New York: Longman.

Hawkesworth, M. E. (1990) *Beyond Oppression: Feminist Theory and Political Strategy*, New York: Continuum.

Hekman, S. (1992) *Gender and Knowledge: Elements of a Postmodern Feminism*, Boston: Northeastern University Press.

Hennessy, R. (1993) *Materialist Feminism and the Politics of Discourse*, London: Routledge.

Hirschmann, N. (1992) *Rethinking Obligation*, London: Cornell University Press.

Homans, H. (1985) *The Sexual Politics of Reproduction*, Aldershot: Gower Publishing.

Hubbard, R. (1990) *The Politics of Women's Biology*, New Brunswick: Rutgers University Press.

Humm, M. (1989) *The Dictionary of Feminist Thought*, London: Harvester Wheatsheaf.

—— (1992) *Feminisms: A Reader*, London: Harvester Wheatsheaf.

Huyssen, A. (1986) *After the Great Divide: Modernism, Mass Culture, Postmodernism*, Bloomington: Indiana University Press.

Irigaray, L. (1985) *Speculum of the Other Woman*, Ithaca: Cornell University Press.

Jackson, L. and Wapner, R. J. (1993) 'Chorionic Villus Sampling' in J. Simpson and S. Elias (eds) *Essentials of Prenatal Diagnosis*, New York: Churchill Livingstone, 45–61.

Jackson, S. (1992) 'The Amazing Deconstructing Woman', *Trouble and Strife*, 25: 25–31.

Jaggar, A. M. (1983) *Feminist Politics and Human Nature*, Brighton: Harvester.

Jaggar, A. and Bordo, S. (eds) (1989) *Gender/Body/Knowledge: Feminist Reconstructions of Being and Knowing*, New Brunswick: Rutgers University Press.

Jagose, A. (1997) '"Feminism without Women": A Lesbian Reassurance' in D. Heller (ed.) *Cross Purposes: Lesbians, Feminists and the Limits of Alliance*, Bloomington and Indianapolis: Indiana University Press, 124–135.

Katz-Rothman, B. (1988) *The Tentative Pregnancy: Prenatal Diagnosis and the Future of Motherhood*, London: Pandora.

Keller, E. F. (1985) *Reflections on Gender and Science*, London: Yale University Press.

Kingston, H. M. (1989) 'Prenatal Diagnosis', *The British Medical Journal*, 298: 1368–1371.

Klein, Renate (1990) 'Genetic & Reproductive Engineering – The Global View', in J. Scutt (ed.) *The Body Machine: Reproductive Technology and the Commercialisation of Motherhood*, London: Merlin Press, 235–273.

Koval, R. (1987) 'What Price the Sale of Reproductive Technology?', *Critical Social Policy*, February, 5–19.

Marshall, B. L. (1994) *Engendering Modernity: Feminism, Social Theory and Social Change*, Oxford: Polity Press.

Martin, E. (1998) 'The Fetus as Intruder: Mothers' Bodies and Medical Metaphors' in R. Davis-Floyd and J. Dumit (eds) *Cyborg Babies*, New York and London: Routledge, 125–142.

McClure, K. (1992) 'The Issue of Foundations: Scientized Politics, Politicized Science, and Feminist Critical Practice' in J. Butler and J. W. Scott (eds) *Feminists Theorize the Political*, London: Routledge, 341–368.

Mies, M. (1993) 'New Reproductive Technologies: Sexist and Racist Implications' in M. Mies and V. Shiva (eds) *Ecofeminism*, London: Zed Books, 174–197.

Mill, J. S. [1869] (1970) 'The Subjection of Women' in Alice Rossi (ed.) *Essays on Sex Equality*, Chicago: University of Chicago Press, 125–242.

Mitchell, J. (1966) 'Women: The Longest Revolution' in *New Left Review*, (Nov./Dec.), 40.

—— (1974) *Psychoanalysis and Feminism*, London: Allen Lane.

Mitchell, L. and Georges, E. (1987) 'Cross-Cultural Cyborgs: Greek and Canadian Women's Discourses on Fetal Ultrasound' in *Feminist Studies*, 23, 2: 373–401.

—— (1998) 'Baby's First Picture: The Cyborg Fetus of Ultrasound Imaging', in R. David-Floyd and J. Dumit (eds) *Cyborg Babies*, New York and London: Routledge, 105–124.

Morgan, R. (1977) *Going Too Far: The Personal Chronicle of a Feminist*, New York: Random House.

*Newsweek* (1993) 'Do All Babies Need Sonograms?', 27 September: 1993, 53.

Nietzsche, F. (1961) *Thus Spoke Zarathustra*, trans. R. J. Hollingdale. Harmondsworth: Penguin Books.

—— (1964) *Beyond Good and Evil*, trans. Helen Zimmern. In *Complete Works*, vol. 12, ed. Oscar Levy, New York: Russell & Russell.

—— (1984) *Human, All Too Human*, Lincoln: University of Nebraska Press.

Nye, A. (1988) *Feminist Theory and the Philosophies of Man*, London: Routledge.

Oakley, A. (1998) 'Science, Gender, and Women's Liberation: An Argument against Postmodernism' in *Women's Studies International Forum* 21, 2: 133–146.

O'Brien, M. (1981) *The Politics of Reproduction*, London: Routledge.

Okin, S. M. (1989) *Justice, Gender and the Family*, New York: Basic Books.

Pateman, C. (1989) *The Disorder of Women*, Oxford: Polity Press.

Petchesky, R. P. (1986) *Abortion and Women's Choice*, London: Verso.

Pollock, S. (1985) 'Sex and the Contraceptive Act', in H. Homans (ed.) *The Sexual Politics of Reproduction*, Aldershot: Gower, 64–77.

Price, D. (1997) *Without a Woman to Read*, Albany: State University of New York Press.

Rabinow, P. (ed.) (1991) *The Foucault Reader: An Introduction to Foucault's Thought*, London: Penguin.

Rapp, R. (1985) 'XYLO: A True Story' in R. Arditti, D. Klein and S. Minden (eds) *Test-Tube Women: What Future for Motherhood?*, London: Pandora, 313–328.

Raymond, J. (1990) 'Of Ice and Men: The Big Chill over Women's Reproductive Rights', *Issues in Reproductive and Genetic Engineering*, 3, 1: 45–50.

—— (1993) *Women as Wombs: Reproductive Technologies and the Battle over Women's Freedom*, San Francisco: HarperCollins.

Reid, M. (1990) 'Pre-natal Diagnosis and Screening', in J. Garcia, R. Kilpatrick and M. Richards (eds) *The Politics of Maternity Care*, Oxford: Clarendon Press, 300–324.

Rich, A. (1977) *Of Woman Born: Motherhood as Experience and Institution*, London: Virago.

——(1986) 'Compulsory Heterosexuality and Lesbian Existence' in *Blood, Bread and Poetry: Selected Prose, 1979–1985*, New York: W. W. Norton, 23–68.

Riley, D. (1988) *Am I That Name?: Feminism and the Category of 'Women' in History*, Basingstoke: Macmillan.

Rorty, R. (1982) *The Consequences of Pragmatism*, Minneapolis: University of Minnesota Press.

—— (1983) 'Postmodernist Bourgeois Liberalism', *Journal of Philosophy*, 80: 583–589.

Rothman, B. K. (1988) *The Tentative Pregnancy*, London: Pandora.

—— (1989) *Recreating Motherhood: Ideology and Technology in a Patriarchal Society*, New York: Norton.

Rousseau, J.-J. [1762] (1955) *Émile*, trans. B. Foxley. London: Dent.

Rowland, R. (1992) *Living Laboratories: Women and Reproductive Technologies*, Bloomington: Indiana University Press.

Royal College of Physicians (1989) *Prenatal Diagnosis and Genetic Screening. Community and Service Implications*, London: RCOP.

Rushdie, S. (1988) *The Satanic Verses*, London: Viking.

Rushing, B. and Onorato, S. (1989) 'Controlling the Means of Reproduction: Feminist Theories and Reproductive Technologies', *Humanity and Society*, 13, 3: 268–291.

Sabbagha, Rudy E. (1993) 'Ultrasound Diagnosis of Fetal Structural Abnormalities', in J. Simpson and S. Elias (eds) *Essentials of Prenatal Diagnosis*, New York: Churchill Livingstone, 91–138.

Saunders, J. and Platt, L. (1997) 'Brains on Toast: the Inexact Science of Gender' in J. Terry and M. Calvert (eds) *Processed Lives: Gender and Technology in Everyday Life*, London: Routledge, 175–180.

Saussure, F. de (1974) *Course in General Linguistics*, London: Fontana.

Sawicki, J. (1991) *Disciplining Foucault: Feminism, Power and the Body*, London: Routledge.

Scheman, N. (1993) *Engenderings: Constructions of Knowledge, Authority, and Privilege*, London: Routledge.

Scholes, R. (1989) 'Eperon Strings', *Differences*, 1: 93–104.

Scott, J. (1993) 'The Tip of the Volcano', *Comparative Study of Society and History*, 438–443.

Scutt, J. (ed.) (1990) *The Body Machine: Reproductive Technology and the Commercialisation of Motherhood*, London: Merlin Press.

Segal, L. (1987) *Is the Future Female? Troubled Thoughts on Contemporary Feminism*, London: Virago.

Shildrick, M. (1997) *Leaky Bodies and Boundaries: Feminism, Postmodernism and Bioethics*, London: Routledge.

Simpson, J. and Elias, S. (eds) (1993) *Essentials of Prenatal Diagnosis*, New York: Churchill Livingstone.

Smith, D. (1987) *The Everyday World as Problematic: A Feminist Sociology*, Milton Keynes: Open University Press.

Solanas, V. (1968) *S.C.U.M. Society for Cutting Up Men Manifesto*, New York: Olympia Press.

Spallone, P. (1989) *Beyond Conception: The New Politics Of Reproduction*, London: Macmillan.

Spiby, J. (1987) *Introduction to Screening for Genetic and Fetal Abnormality*, London: King's Fund Centre.

Squier, S. (1996) 'Fetal Subjects and Maternal Objects: Reproductive Technology and the New Fetal/Maternal Relation', *Journal of Medicine and Philosophy*, 21: 5.

Stabile, C. A. (1994) *Feminism and the Technological Fix*, Manchester: Manchester University Press.

Stanworth, M. (1987) *Reproductive Technologies: Gender, Motherhood and Medicine*, Oxford: Polity Press.

Steinberg, D. (ed.) (1996) *Border Patrols: Policing Sexual Boundaries*, London: Cassell.

Sutton, A. (1990) *Prenatal Diagnosis: Confronting the Ethical Issues*, London: Linacre Centre for the Study of the Ethics of Health Care.

Taylor, H. [1851] (1970) 'Enfranchisement of Women', in Alice Rossi (ed.) *Essays on Sex Equality*, Chicago: University of Chicago Press, 89–121.

Thompson, D. (1996) 'The Self-contradiction of "Postmodernist" Feminism' in D. Bell and R. Klein (eds) *Radically Speaking: Feminism Reclaimed*, London: Zed Books, 325–338.

Tietung Hospital of Anshan Iron and Steel Co. (1975) 'Fetal Sex Prediction by Sex Chromatin of Chorionic Villi Cells during Early Pregnancy', *Chinese Medical Journal*, 1: 117.

Tong, R. (1989) *Feminist Thought: A Comprehensive Introduction*, London: Unwin Hyman.

Tuana, N. (ed) (1989) *Feminism and Science*, Bloomington: Indiana University Press.

Ussher, J. (1991) *Women's Madness: Misogyny or Mental Illness?*, Amherst, PA: University of Massachusetts Press.

Walby, S. (1990) *Theorizing Patriarchy*, Oxford: Basil Blackwell.

Wald, N. (1984) 'Conclusions', in N. Wald (ed.) *Antenatal and Neonatal Screening*, Oxford: Oxford University Press, 537–551.

Warnock, M. (1985) *Aspects of Life: The Warnock Report on Human Fertilisation and Embryology*, Oxford: Basil Blackwell.

Warren, M. A. (1985) *Gendercide*, New Jersey: Rowan & Allanheld.

Waters, K. (1996) '(Re)Turning to the Modern: Radical Feminism and the Post-modern Turn' in D. Bell and R. Klein (eds) *Radically Speaking: Feminism Reclaimed*, London: Zed Books, 280–296.

Weedon, C. (1987) *Feminist Practice and Poststructuralist Theory*, Oxford: Basil Blackwell.

Weeks, K. (1998) *Constituting Feminist Subjects*, Ithaca: Cornell University Press.

Whelehan, I. (1995) *Modern Feminist Thought*, Edinburgh: Edinburgh University Press.

Whitford, M. (1991) *Luce Irigaray: Philosophy in the Feminine*, London: Routledge.

Whittle, M. J. and Connor, J. M. (eds) (1989) *Prenatal Diagnosis in Obstetric Practice*, Oxford: Blackwell Scientific Publications.

Wollstonecraft, M. [1792] (1975) *Vindication of the Rights of Woman*, ed. Miriam Brody, London: Penguin.

Yeatman, A. (1994) *Postmodern Revisionings of the Political*, London: Routledge.

# Index

abortion: of abnormal foetuses 88,
  90, 114–15; of female babies in
  India 100; and prenatal screening
  84–6, 88
'affirmative action' 8
Alcoff, L. 29
alphafetoprotein 143
amniocentesis 78, 98, 100, 143
Aristotle 24
Ashley, K. 107, 116, 119–20, 124,
  135, 136, 1123
Attwood, M. see Handmaid's Tale

Bacon, F. 14
Baines, E. see Birth Machine, The
Barrett, M. and Phillips, A. 29, 72,
  138
beauty, female 43
behaviour: interest in biological
  bases of 85
Bell, D. and Klein, R. 76
Birth Machine, The (Baines) 124–5,
  126
body, working of 34–5
Brooks, A. 29
Bruckner, P. see Divine Child, The
Butler, J. 1, 2, 43, 131, 136, 142
Butler, J. and Scott, J.W. 69, 130

Campbell, B. 138
capitalism: constraining nature of
  structure of 83, 108; female body
  as site of profit-making 84; and
  patriarchy 17–18; and science 83,
  87, 88, 91

Carder, A. 94–5
Cartesian thought 25, 34, 35, 39
Catholic Church 68
childlessness 77, 78, 106–7, 110,
  134
Chile 57
China 96, 97
Chodorow, N. 19
chorionic villus sampling (CVS) 144
chromosomes 35, 143
class: and gender 16–17
Clomid 82
clomiphene citrate 81
Clough, P.T. 29
coal miners' strike (1984/85) 61
consciousness-raising 50
contraceptive pill 102
cordocentesis 144
Corea, G. 15, 80
Coward, R. see Sacred Cows

Daly, M. 11, 18, 92
de Beauvoir, S. 70
decision-making 89
deconstruction 22, 27, 32, 39, 43, 56,
  66, 68, 106, 109, 112–13, 130, 135,
  137
deconstructive feminism 27
Derrida, J. 60, 61
Descartes, R. 23, 34, 36, 67
Di Stefano, C. 33
'disciplinary practices' 117
discrimination: physiological and
  emotional justifications for gender
  8–9

*Divine Child, The* (Bruckner) 121–2, 137
doctors: attitude towards women 79
Down's Syndrome 88, 115–16, 144
dual-systems: versus unified systems debate 17, 18
dualisms 46–7, 50, 56, 62, 139
Dworkin, A. 1, 2, 3, 4, 15, 18, 96, 99, 136, 142

education 7, 48
Elam, D. 38, 41
employment: and motherhood 90
Enlightenment 72; and modernist feminism 23, 67, 71, 139–40; postmodern feminist distrust of progressive values of 54, 57, 65, 67
epistemology 67; feminist standpoint 19–20, 50–4, 61; foundations for knowledge-building 46; importance of knowledge as tool to understand ourselves 48; knowledge as progressive force 47; and modernist feminism 44–54, 61, 71–2, 128; and modernist feminism in context of reproductive technologies 87–97, 103–4; and objectivity 47; and postmodern feminism 25–6, 54, 55–62; and postmodern feminism in context of reproductive technologies 116–22; power and knowledge 55, 56, 57–8, 71; and radical feminism 48–50, 72, 104, 140
Equal Pay Act (1970) 7, 32
equal pay and opportunities 7, 34, 63
eugenics 85, 145

Farquhar, D. 126
*Female Eunuch, The* (Greer) 10, 15
Feminist International Network of Resistance to Reproductive and Genetic Engineering (FINRRAGE) (was FINNRET) 101

*Feminist Review* (journal) 20
feminist standpoint epistemology 19–20, 50–4, 61
Ferguson, K. 36
fetoscopy 145
Fitzsimons, L. 10, 11
Flax, J. 30–1, 68, 70
foetus: control of 120–2; definition 145; positioning as subject though ultrasound 120; separation from maternal body through reproductive technologies 95–6, 124
Foucault, M. 26, 57–8, 117, 131
France 7
Freud, S. 18
Friedan, B. 4, 7

Gardiner, J.K. 18
Gatens, M. 29
gender 19, 41, 97; and class 16–17; hierarchy of 47, 50, 90
genes 35, 85
Gilligan, C. 19, 89–90
Gilman, C.P. *see Socialist and the Suffragist, The*
girls: 'engendered' from early age 19
Gouges, O. de 7
Grant, J. 26
Greer, G. *see Female Eunuch, The*
Griffin, S. 50

*Handmaid's Tale* (Attwood) 141
Harding, S. 53
Hartsock, N. 53
Harvard Medical School 8
Hekman, S. 64
heterosexuality 112–13
hierarchy: and dualisms 47, 50, 62, 90
Hindley, M. 42
Hitler, A. 115
homosexuality: and genes 35, 85; lesbian women and IVF 114

identity politics 33, 63–4, 69, 77
in vitro fertilisation *see* IVF
India 96–7, 100
Irigaray, L. 70

IVF (in-vitro fertilisation) 77, 81–3, 96; 'assaultive' process 81, 86; and discrimination 113–14; emotional and psychological effects 82–3; glossary term 145; harmful effects of drugs 81–2; and lesbian women 114; low success rate 82; personal experiences of 106–7, 108; postmodernist perspectives on 109–10, 133–4

Jagger, A. 2, 14, 20
Jagose, A. 29
*Junior* (film) 99
justice, principles of 35

Klein, R. 91
'knowing self' 36, 37, 46
knowledge *see* epistemology
Kohlberg, L. 89–90

language: and postmodern feminism 25, 56, 60; and Saussure 25, 60
Leeds Reproductive Rights Group 100–1
lesbians 20; and IVF 114
liberal feminism 3, 5–10, 11, 64; advantages of 140; concepts of 5–6; and epistemology 48, 71, 87, 103; and gender discrimination 8; 'getting into the game' 65; goals of 6; gulf between socialist/radical feminism and 132–3; men and women should be treated the same assertion 6, 7–8, 37, 38, 65, 102, 131; and motherhood 108; reaction to 9–10; and reproductive technologies 78–9, 101, 102–3, 131–2; *see also* modernist feminism
Locke, J. 7

male violence 1; and radical feminism 14, 15, 20
Marshall, B.L. 20
Marx, K. 72
Marxism 18, 26, 86–7; and socialist feminism 17, 21
medical profession: attitude towards women 79

Mill, H.T. 7
Mill, J.S. 7, 48
Mitchell, J. *see* 'Women: The Longest Revolution'
modernist feminism: and agency 38; aim to improve women's lives 128; characteristics 129; and Enlightenment 23, 67, 71, 139–40; and epistemology 44–54, 61, 71–2, 128; and epistemology in context of reproductive technologies 87–97, 103–4; fears of postmodernists 31; and 'getting it right' 35; gulf between different feminisms 132–3; and her-story 36–7; making women's lives better 34–6; and motherhood 108; and politics 63–6, 69, 71, 122, 130–1, 131–2, 137; and politics in context of reproductive technologies 97–102, 103; and reproductive technologies 75–104; seen as 'virtually useless' and anachronistic 3, 73, 130, 139, 142; and subject of woman 32–9, 40–1, 44, 63, 69; and subject of women in context of reproductive technologies 76–87, 102, 103; and theory 130; and truth 33, 35–6, 44–5, 47–8, 57, 59, 87, 128; *see also* liberal feminism; radical feminism; socialist feminism
moral reasoning 19, 89
motherhood 90, 107, 108, 134, 135; and employment 90; experiences of 107, 108, 111; modernist feminist readings of 108, 134; and radical feminists 108

'naming' 59–60, 60–1
National Health Service *see* NHS
National Organisation for Women (NOW) 7–8
Nazi regime 81, 85
neural tube defects 145–6
New York Redstockings 11
NHS (National Health Service) 53
Nietzsche, F. 61
nurses 53

Oakley, A. 75
objectivity: and knowledge 47
Oedipus conflict 19
Okin, S.M. 8
oppression, women's 18, 73, 130
Orme, M. 115–16

Paine, T. 7
patriarchy 50, 108; and capitalism
   17–18; definition 11–12; radical
   feminists' view of 11–12, 16, 18,
   38, 42, 81, 83, 132; and science 83,
   87, 88, 91
Perganol 82
pill, contraceptive 102
Pinochet, General 57
Plato 24
politics 137–8, 141; differences
   between modernist and
   postmodernist 130–2; and
   modernist feminism 63–6, 69, 71,
   122, 130–1, 131–2, 137; and
   modernist feminism in context of
   reproductive technologies 97–102,
   103; and postmodern feminism
   67–70, 71, 130, 131; and
   postmodern feminism in context
   of reproductive technologies 122–6
postmodern feminism 22–8; aims of
   73, 130; alleged inaccessibility of
   22; arbitrariness of meanings 25;
   and category of woman 22–4, 26,
   40; criticism of totalising theories
   26–7; and deconstruction of
   women 39, 56, 66, 68, 69, 131;
   destabilisation of subject in
   context of reproductive
   technologies 106–16; distrust of
   progressive values of the
   Enlightenment 54, 57, 65, 67;
   dominance of 3; and epistemology
   25–6, 54, 55–62; and epistemology
   in context of reproductive
   technologies 116–22; fears of by
   modernists and responses to 31;
   features 22, 27; hostility towards
   30–1; and language 25, 56, 60; and
   politics 67–70, 71, 130, 131; and
   politics in context of reproductive
   technologies 122–6; and power 26,

67–8, 131; rejection of women and
   subject 24, 31, 32, 39–44, 128–9;
   and reproductive technologies
   106–27, 133–4; sources 22; and
   theory 129–30
postmodernist–modernist gulf 3, 4,
   71–3, 128–42; doubts over 132–8;
   over politics 130–2; over theory
   128–30; recovering of 138–40;
   similarities 132, 135
poststructural feminism 3
power: Foucault on 57–8; and
   knowledge 55, 56, 57–8, 71 and
   postmodern feminism 26, 67–8,
   131; and truth 59
pregnancy 93
pregnant body, duality of 123–4
prenatal screening 91, 96, 114–15,
   138; and abortion 84–6, 88;
   glossary term 146; knowledge and
   understanding of 88–9; and liberal
   feminism 58; negative implications
   for women 93; overlooking of
   emotional implications by medical
   profession 98; purpose of 84;
   *see also* amniocentesis; ultrasound
prenatal sex determination 100
Price, D. 30, 75, 102, 142
private: and public spheres 52, 64
privilege: and knowledge 55–6
psychoanalysis 18

'Quaker Oats Box Man' image 41–2,
   60

Rabinow, P. 71
radical feminism 10–16, 27, 80, 96;
   associated with female
   victimisation and male violence
   13, 15, 20; concepts and features
   of 10–11; and control 80; and
   epistemology 48–50, 72, 104, 140;
   and 'getting into the game' 65–6;
   and motherhood 108; and
   patriarchy 11–12, 16, 18, 38, 42,
   81, 83, 132; placing of women at
   the centre 12–13, 16, 37;
   representations of 10; reproductive
   technologies seen as threat 96,
   100–1, 103, 132; and science 14;

successes 15; susceptibility in being
dismissed as outdated 14–15;
ultimate goal 132; *see also*
modernist feminism
Raymond, J. 94
'reclaim the night' marches 64
Redstockings 11
reductionism 35
reproductive technologies 4–5;
control and manipulation of
women's bodies through 78, 80,
91, 132; destabilisation of subject
by postmodern feminism in
context of 106–16; development
within structures of capitalism and
patriarchy 83, 84, 87, 88, 92; envy
by men of woman's power to give
birth 92–3, 99; epistemology and
modernist feminism in context of
87–97, 103–4; epistemology and
postmodern feminism in context
of 116–22; and erasure of women
92–3, 94; fear of losing power of
birth by modernist feminists
99–100, 108; female reproductive
body as site of profit 83–4, 91;
fragmentation and
dismemberment of women 91–2,
93, 95–7; increasing use of
machines and implications 94-5;
and modernist feminism 75–104;
placing motherhood under control
of men 96; politics and modernist
feminism in context of 97–102,
103; politics and postmodern
feminism in context of 122–6; and
postmodern feminism 106–27; and
reproduction of the 'legitimate
sexual and reproducing subject'
113–16; resistance to and seen as a
threat by radical feminists 96,
100–1, 103, 132; seen as providing
more options for women by liberal
feminists 101, 103; and separation
of foetus from maternal body
95–6; subject and modernist
feminism in context of 76–87, 102,
103; *see also* IVF; prenatal
screening; ultrasound

reverse discrimination 8
Rich, A. 107, 113
Rousseau, J.-J. 6, 24
Royal College of Physicians:
*Prenatal Diagnosis* report
115–16

*Sacred Cows* (Coward) 138, 139
Saussure, F. de 25, 60
Scheman, N. 36, 66
science 47; growth of modern 35;
and ideologies of capitalism and
patriarchy 83, 87, 88, 91; and
masculinity 14, 92
self-discipline 118
sex determination: of babies 100
Sex Discrimination Act (1975) 7,
32
sex pre-selection 96
signs 60
*Silent Scream, A* (film) 120
single mother 113
slavery 58–9, 81
Smith, D. 53
socialist feminism 3, 16–22, 37, 80,
132; aims 20; assessment of
usefulness 21; dual-systems theory
verses unified systems theory
17–18; and epistemology 50–1,
71–2, 104; features and concepts
of 17; and gendered differences 19;
and 'getting into the game' 65;
and Marxism 17, 21; and
psychoanalysis 18–19; and racism
20; and reproductive technologies
132; and sexuality 20; successes
21–2; tensions between class and
gender 16–17; *see also* modernist
feminism
*Socialist and the Suffragist, The*
(Gilman) 16, 65
Solanas, V. 11
Stabile, C.A. 94
standpoint theory *see* feminist
standpoint epistemology
Stanton, E.C. 7
Stanworth, M. 85
Steptoe, P. 114
story-telling 123

subject: destabilisation of by
    postmodern feminism in context
    of reproductive technologies
    106–16; and modernist feminism
    32–9, 40–1, 44, 63, 69; and
    modernist feminism in context of
    reproductive technologies 76–87,
    102, 103; rejection of by
    postmodern feminism 24, 31, 32,
    39–44, 128–9
suffragettes 9, 42, 87

Taylor, D. 97
'tentative pregnancy' syndrome 93
test-tube babies *see* IVF
theory 19, 73; different ideas about
    129–30; and modernist feminism
    129; and postmodern feminism
    129–30
toxic waste disposal 62
truth 67; Foucault on 58; and
    language 60; and man 47, 48; and
    modernist feminism 33, 35–6,
    44–5, 47–8, 57, 59, 87, 128; and
    postmodern feminism 55, 57, 62
Truth, Sojourner 22–3

ultrasound 78, 95, 118–20, 123,
    135–6; effects of 119–20; glossary
    term 146–7; market 84;
    positioning of foetus as subject
    through 120; visual erasure of
    women through 94
unified systems theorists 18
United States 7, 21

*Warnock Report* 110
Weedon, C. 111
Widdecombe, A. 24–5
Wollstonecraft, M. 6–7, 9–10, 24, 48
*Woman's Hour* 138
women: infinite representations of
    41–2, 43; psychological differences
    between men and 89
'Women: The Longest Revolution'
    (Mitchell) 18